HOME

THE NEW SOCIAL

Subkultura

STORIES OF YOUTH AND RESISTANCE IN RUSSIA 1815–2017

by Artemy Troitsky

ISBN 978-0-9929524-8-8

Author: Artemy Troitsky
Editor: Jamie Rann
Managing Editor & Compiler: Olya Sova

Translation: Jamie Rann, Felix White-Thomson, Julie Butler, Anya Harrison
Proofreading: Alice Lewis
Design: Juris Petraskevics
Illustrations editor: Oxana Polyakova
Initial illustrations research: Sasha Moroz
Fact checking: Irina Oznobikhina
Editorial consultants: Thomas Phongsathorn, Fred Harrison

Production: The New Social in association with HOME
Distribution: Cornerhouse Publications

Print: JELGAVAS TIPOGRĀFIJA

Distribution worldwide: Cornerhouse Publications
www.cornerhousepublications.org

HOME

THE NEW SOCIAL

FOREWORD

JON SAVAGE

When I was researching my book *Teenage*, I came across an extraordinary book by an author simply called Voinov, *Outlaw: The Autobiography of a Soviet Waif.* Inside, the first hand account told a terrible story of one facet of Russian society in the 1930s, concentrating on the effects of the purges and the Holodomor – the Soviet famine of 1932–33 that resulted in up to ten million deaths. I couldn't believe what I was reading.

When his engineer father was purged in 1929, Kolya – as he is addressed in the book – is placed, at the age of six, in an orphanage full of "tattered and filthy" children. After a few years, his initial terror turns into toughness and indifference: "each of us felt that he was an outcast, that ordinary normal living was impossible for him, that the outside world had become alien and hostile. One had to struggle to survive, and only those succeeded who ruthlessly fought for the right to live".

Voinov's attitude hardens: "I began to understand my waif comrades – their sullenness, bitterness and hatred, their suspicion of everyone else outside their own world. For the first time in my life, I felt the chasm separating me, as a waif, from all the people who did not live as I did. It became clear to me that the waifs were my friends, my family, and that I would have to stick to them or die." Befriended by some adolescents, he embarks on a course of petty theft and violence – a young Artful Dodger taught the tricks of his new trade by Fagins like his older friend Mishka.

"In the winter of 1932–33 our 'work' became increasingly difficult and dangerous; we had to use more resourcefulness than ever before. I had acquired a hunting knife, and always wore it up my sleeve, strapped to my wrist. This was a time when a stolen chunk of bread could cost you your life and hardly any of us ventured out unarmed. The once crowded marketplaces were now almost empty. A few beetroots and a rare roll, half flour, half sawdust, were displayed on the stalls. Starving, we acted with desperate recklessness… Hundreds of waifs tramped the streets, gathered near the railway stations, died under the hedges…"

This story introduced to the triumph and the tragedy of Soviet Russia's youth. I was unable to use the material in *Teenage* because time and space demanded that I keep my story to America, the UK, and Northern Europe but in *Subkultura* Artemy Troitsky has filled in a complete history of Russian youth, from the Decembrists of the mid-nineteenth century to the Nihilists to the eager revolutionaries of the early twentieth century, the official state youth group, the Komsomol, and the young dissidents who had to navigate a system that became ever more oppressive.

You can tell a lot about a country by the way it treats its youth. Troitsky details the ritual dance that has existed in Russia between at first monarchic and then state control, and the basic human desire for freedom: he insists on subcultures because when people come together they have more power. Today he feels that the many types of Russian youth – the hipsters, the *gopniks* (hooligans) – have returned to a kind of apathy and hopelessness that echoes the state of their forebears in the mid-nineteenth century, with a future that is "so empty, dark and cold".

How the past informs the present, how patterns keep recurring, that is Troitsky's theme. Yet he insists that change has to happen – because the other way is stasis, entropy, death. In his afterword, he celebrates the person (usually young) who "is simply the first person to 'break through the ice', to make the decisive step that the crowd has been waiting for nervously, which will make them charge in one direction or another with rapid force". There is always hope.

Passport photo, circa 1990.
Courtesy of the author

"We tried our best, but it's the same old mess." This phrase has become a folk saying in Russia. First uttered by former prime minister Viktor Chernomyrdin in 1993, it gives an exhaustive description of Russia's fate, combining lofty aspiration and desultory results. Admittedly, I'm not sure that Russia's current leaders are genuinely trying their best – not for anything other than their own bank balance, certainly – but right now it looks like we've ended up with the same old mess again. Once more Russia is the epicentre of bad news: military aggression, absurd new laws, persecuted dissidents, dodgy secret service manoeuvres and man-made catastrophes, not to mention an economic crisis and declining living standards. The reaction of so-called "ordinary Russians" to all this is hardly cause for celebration either. At best, they respond with weak-willed apathy; more often they choose to participate in a pageant of patriotic euphoria. The perennial rollercoaster of Russian public life is currently on a headlong descent. Those of us on board have our eyes screwed shut and no idea how long we'll be falling for.

There is probably no other nation that has experienced such bad luck with its leaders as Russia – a procession of madmen, tyrants, thieves, and power-crazy philistines. And nowhere have leaders had as much luck with their citizens – patient, naïve, intimidated and obedient. In a country with a centuries-old tradition of slavery, only brought to an end one hundred and fifty years ago, it might seem that absolutely nothing can be done for a population raised on injustice and fear.

But there have always been people who have tried to disperse the storm clouds. Occasionally they have been successful, even if not for long. Russia is the perfect country for rebels because there is always something to rebel against. These revolutionaries, dissidents and conspirators have always had a practical goal: to change the country for the better, to get the rollercoaster of Russia heading up. Almost every time they meet with defeat because there is no solution for the task at hand. The favourite toast of Soviet dissidents was "To the success of our lost cause!"

In this way, making the world a better place stopped being a universal, practical cause and became something personal and existential. To resist slavery and to live free! To resist hypocrisy and to live honestly. To resist fear and to live courageously. "Live not by lies," as Alexander Solzhenitsyn once said. And, despite the oppression weighing down over the last two hundred years, there have been millions of young Russian men and women who have followed this path. And it is these young people and the subcultures they created that this book is about.

Why only the young? That's just how it happened. It's probably because young people never realise how hard their task really is. Many of them died trying, although some did manage to live to a wise old age. The desperate heroes of the past find their successors in each new generation and it is thanks to them that Russia hasn't yet become a kingdom of utter darkness and our little rollercoaster can still sometimes shoot upwards and pause at the summit for a single happy moment.

I decided to write this book because I felt the state of Russia today compelled me to. We are currently experiencing a period of darkness – one that for many people seems to be without hope. I can see my friends' children leaving Russia one by one. And even my own children don't plan on staying here for long. There was a time when I dreamed of writing a gentle, fatherly book for them about this vast country that I love so dearly. But I can't do that right now. The story this book will tell will be different: unsentimental, even frightening. But maybe it will be inspiring too – and that's why I have to write it.

I hope that finding out a bit about my life will help you understand why I am the person to tell the story of two centuries of subcultures in Russia, especially when it comes to the last fifty years.

I was born in 1955 – the same year, just about, as rock and roll – and this coincidence seems to have had a significant impact on my life. But it wasn't until the following decade that I first heard about Elvis. In the meantime, I had started school in Moscow and, at seven years old, had joined the Communist youth group, the 'Little Octobrists'. At school, I wore a little red badge in the shape of a star with a tiny portrait of Lenin in the middle and I knew off by heart all the songs about the October Revolution and its leader. I can still sing some now:

Wearing Cuban revolutionary uniform brought by Dad from Havana, 1962. Courtesy of the author

> When Lenin was a little lad
> With shiny golden curls,
> Cosy little boots he had
> Like other boys and girls.

But it was as a faithful Little Octobrist that I first heard rock and roll – this music from another world. I was lucky: I caught the bug a lot earlier than my Soviet peers because in 1963 I went to live in Prague with my parents. My mum and dad were born in the late 1920s and were representatives of the Soviet intelligentsia of the Sixties in all its glory. The best years of their lives coincided with the denunciation of Stalin and the easing of censorship under Khrushchev, with the era of Sputnik, Gagarin and the Cuban Revolution. They were sincere young intellectuals and communists who believed in 'Socialism with a human face' until reality forced them to take a more cynical view. I loved them very much but, unfortunately, they didn't like my sort of music at all. My mum listened to Mozart and my dad to revolutionary anthems. He was one of the first Soviet citizens to fly to Cuba after the revolution, where he met Fidel Castro and Che Guevara. The death of Che in the autumn of 1967 was my first family tragedy, the first time I felt true grief. But it was when Soviet tanks rolled into Czechoslovakia in August 1968 that our happy family was really broken apart. The spark of enthusiasm in my father's eyes died that day. He was 40 years old.

At the age of nine I graduated from the Octobrists into the ranks of the Young Pioneers. This was a more serious organisation altogether – a sort of Communist Scouts with its own charter and oath and summer camps with kids lining up under the red flag. I hadn't been in the Pioneers long – just three years – before I was thrown out for playing Western music in the school radio room. But, after being sent away to another school, I was soon tying on the 'Pioneers' little red neckerchief again as if nothing had happened. The second time I was excluded for something more serious: anti-Soviet propaganda. I had been extolling the virtues of 'Socialism with a human face' to my fellow students and had described the Soviet intervention in Czechoslovakia as a disgrace. One of my classmates informed on me. It was lucky I was only 13 years old, or the consequences would have been much more severe. I never spoke out so naively again, but I did start nursing a grudge against the Soviet authorities.

I didn't become a political activist, however: there was no movement I could have joined back then in that unthinking, ignorant era. But I did find a community of like-minded people in the so-called 'internal emigration' movement. We, the kids of the Soviet subcultures – the Beatlemaniacs, the rockers, the hippies – were physically present in the streets of Moscow and Leningrad, studying and working beneath posters of Lenin and Brezhnev, listening to Communist incantations on the news and other such totalitarian rubbish. But in our hearts and souls we soared in a perfect world filled with Lennon, Hendrix and Marley; in our minds we splashed among the puddles of Woodstock and basked in the Californian sun. It was as part of this community that in 1972 I became to all intents and purposes Moscow's first ever DJ. Two years later, my disco was closed down by the Komsomol, the Soviet Union's official youth organisation, for being ideologically subversive. This harsh encounter with reality was painful but did little to stop those of us looking for some alternative.

Over the following decades this search prompted many transformations: thanks to David Bowie, we swapped our multi-coloured

Little Octobrist badge

flares for austere monochrome and chopped off our hair. In the era of punk and new wave, we became more energetic and increasingly integrated into the world around us. All of a sudden there were bands who sang – in Russian! – about things that were totally unacceptable to officialdom. Handwritten rock zines were circulated along with DIY music recordings. Throughout the 1980s I was completely obsessed with the madness that was Russian Rock, an explosion of underground musical talent and energy. I started out by helping the movement to survive during the death throes of the old Soviet order in the early Eighties. Then, in the short period of 'perestroika and glasnost' under Gorbachev, I worked as a promoter for my favourite artists both within the country and abroad, writing books and making documentaries.

In the early Nineties, however, Russian Rock lost the comforting certainty of the Soviet regime and with it its sense of a common purpose. This identity crisis fatally undermined the movement, which ultimately became part of the entertainment establishment. Soon I found a new plaything – clubs and dance music, organising Gagarin Party, Moscow's first and most notorious rave. My rave period didn't last long, though: the scene was soon taken over by drug dealers and gangsters and one of my business partners was killed. I immersed myself in television work instead, working from 1991 to 1994 as the head of music at a state TV channel. But it soon became very evident that ratings and bribes were a lot more important to TV insiders than quality so I decided to wave goodbye to this cultural revolution and accepted an offer from America to launch a Russian version of *Playboy*, maintaining some connection with television by hosting *Café Oblomov*, a laid-back late-night TV show. I was 40 years old.

Leo Tolstoy's *Anna Karenina* famously starts: "All happy families are alike; every unhappy family is unhappy in its own way." Here's another take: All adults throughout history are alike; every new generation of young people is different in its own way. We can probably take it as read that people aged between, say, 15 and 30 are the most inquisitive and dynamic section of society. They don't yet really know what life is about, but they want to know; they're not satisfied with life but they want satisfaction, be it financial or philosophical; they don't yet know their place in the world but they want to find it – and they want to find others like them. This is what drives young people to join clubs, gangs, tribes, organisations and movements, to turn a passion into a subculture.

This spontaneous collectivism is not typical of adults, largely because the most important thing for the average adult is his or her personal life (however functional or dysfunctional this may be) – family, children, friends, career. But what is there beyond this? What reasons are there to 'get together'? For the younger generation, it's very different. For adults, the impact of the charms of 'real life' – injustice, hypocrisy, stupidity and intolerance – is softened by their own rich experience of

Hippie period: in Gurzuf, Crimea, Summer of 1974. Courtesy of the author

life; the young feel these blows sharply. This gives rise to thoughts which cynical adults prefer to dismiss as idealistic, romantic or just plain stupid: "It's boring," "I want to be different," "We have to change the world!" To truly enjoy life is hard enough, but to bring about change as well is even harder. In fact, it's impossible – if you're trying to do it all on your own. And so restless young people join forces with other like-minded souls and they create their own very varied organisations – from terrorist cells to religious cults to rock groups.

In addition to a general emphasis on the here and now, there are two things necessary for making a subculture. The first is an ideology. The second is a lifestyle. It is this lifestyle which shows the outside world that there is something special about this particular niche group within the overall cultural kaleidoscope. It is a special sort of code which can manifest itself anywhere – in your clothes, your attitude, the slang you use, the books you read, the music you listen to and much else besides. Of course, not every subculture manifests itself in every expression of taste. Looking at examples from this book, for the dandies of the early nineteenth century (Chapter One) it was your attitude and your clothes that mattered most; for the avant-gardists of the early twentieth century it was literature and painting (Chapter Four); for today's hipsters (Chapter Eleven), it's music, cinema and food.

For the majority of subcultures, with the possible exception of anarchists, hippies and patriots (Chapters Four, Seven and Ten), the underlying philosophy is not actually that important. Likewise, subcultures don't really have leaders: there is no sense of hierarchy, no clear goal. Subcultures can be powerful and popular but the one thing they have in common is that their structure is amorphous. Style prevails over content and aesthetics over functionality. What's more, I realised while working on this book that many of the Russian subcultures I was dealing with – the superfluous men (Chapter One), nihilists (Chapter Two) or the 'mitki' (Chapter Ten) – didn't even have a dress code, a favourite hangout or a special slang. They existed not so much on the street as on paper, in the fantasies of writers and analyses of critics. But I refuse to brush them aside because they are vitally important to understanding the story of youth and resistance in Russia. Moreover, as you will see, there have been many cases when these subcultures suddenly and unexpectedly stopped being virtual and became very real.

Also included in this book are some youth movements for whom a profound ideological core is far more important than a look, movements with leaders, structure and objectives. These can come 'from above', with the support of the state, like the Komsomol (Chapter Five), but usually they come from below, as opposition or alternative to the status quo, like the anti-Stalin underground (Chapter Five) or the Marxists (Chapter Three).

In 1937, at the height of Stalin's Terror, a 19-year-old poet named Pavel Kogan wrote a song called *The Brigantine*. Kogan himself was

Russian Rock: with Kino and Joanna Stingray at Nevsky Prospect. Leningrad, 1987. Courtesy of the author

killed in the Second World War, in 1942, but during the brief flowering of freedom that was the Khrushchev Thaw in the late Fifties and early Sixties *The Brigantine* became something of an anthem for young romantics who were, in Kogan's words, "sick of talking and arguing and loving tired eyes". These romantics were known as the children of the Sixties, and they too will be part of our story (Chapter Six). But there is something in Kogan's lyrics which speaks for all the subcultures in this book, for everyone in Russia who has sought their own path in the face of adversity.

> Let's drink to the passionate, the peculiar,
> Those who leave behind a cosy bed,
> To the pirate crews singing shanties
> With the Jolly Roger overhead.

In theory, these lines, conjuring up as they do images of the dying rays of the Caribbean sunset, could have been written anywhere. But, for me, they could only come from Russia. Whenever I used to read books from outside Russia about youth and young people – from the apologetic J.D. Salinger to the apocalyptic William Golding – I always caught myself thinking that there was something a bit different about Russia. Even familiar phenomena with familiar names – dandies, hippies, yuppies – mutated considerably once they arrived here and now bear little resemblance to their forebears. Other movements – surfers, pacifists, anti-globalisation activists – never appeared in Russia, for various reasons, both climatic and political. But then we also had our own homegrown subculture movements which the West simply wouldn't go near.

Throughout this book I have intentionally focused on those subcultures and youth movements that are unique to Russia or ones which, when borrowed from outside, underwent important and significant transformations on Russian soil. I have avoided any in-depth consideration of Russian subcultures that were just unconvincing – and usually less polished – 'copies' of existing Western ones. This applies to a variety of phenomena – from Freemasons and Suffragettes to emos and football hooligans. The book proceeds in an almost entirely chronological fashion from nineteenth-century aristocrats to today's emergent online communities, but this chronology is sometimes broken. Many very diverse strands in the story of youth in Russia took place in parallel: the austere and serious Bolsheviks shared the streets with the decadent and outrageous avant-garde. This diversity, and sometimes the incompatibility of the different forms it took – politics, fashion, philosophy, music, literature, violence – will perhaps make the narrative somewhat uneven, especially when it comes to my own personal memories. But this is inevitable when dealing with a subject that is at once entertaining and deadly serious.

In a sense, this book is an alternative history of Russia of the last two hundred years. 'Alternative' can be understood in two ways. On the one hand it means a new point of view which balances out conventional top-down histories told from the perspective of the state and the handful of men who run it. But it is also alternative because it offers a glimpse of history as seen through the eyes of the young people whose creative, independent, alternative spirit made and continue to make a Russia that is very different from the land of tsars, generals and secret policemen. A glimpse of a history that is just as passionate and peculiar as the people who made it.

Speaking from the stage during a protest against the falsification of parliamentary election results. December 2011, Moscow, Russia. Courtesy of the author

Peter cutting boyars' beards. 1770s.
Caricature on wood

NOBLE FAILURES: Dandies and Decembrists, Superfluous Men and Slavophiles. 1815–1861

The first, and perhaps the greatest, rebel against the traditional Russian way of life was Peter the Great, ruler of Russia from 1682 to 1725. When he came to power, Peter was young and, like the heroes of Kogan's *The Brigantine*, he was passionate and peculiar. Extremely tall and imposing, he didn't even look Russian. He was just 26 when he returned from an eighteen-month tour of northern Europe in 1698 intent on modernising Russia. One of his first acts was to order all men, except the clergy and peasantry, to shave off their beards and to swap their traditional long Tatar-style coats, baggy trousers and boots for a German style of dress – jackets, waistcoats, full-length trousers and shoes.

It is true that Peter's attempt to turn Russia into Holland was a failure – as is evident enough from the current state of the country – because most of his innovations were only superficial. But it was his most superficial reforms that were actually the most effective: the changes he instigated in people's clothes and grooming. We can still see the results of his decree around us, with only the bushy-bearded hipsters spoiling the picture somewhat. What's more, it was Peter who, by founding a new capital in St Petersburg, gave Russia access to all the temptations of Europe, providing inspiration for many subsequent subcultural rebellions.

Catherine the Great. From the series
Life of Fabulous Monroes.
Vladislav Mamyshev-Monroe, 1996.
Courtesy of the Aksenov Family Foundation

Peter the Great. From the series
Life of Fabulous Monroes.
Vladislav Mamyshev-Monroe, 1996.
Courtesy of the Aksenov Family Foundation

Cover page of Pushkin's
Eugene Onegin
by Dmitri Prigov. 1998.
Published by Mitkilibris and
Krasny Matros

Dandies

Despite his unusual achievements, Peter was not Russia's first subcultural hero: he was young and daring but he was also a ruling monarch. But his clothing reforms did sow a subcultural seed. Every subculture is a protest against routine, against the everyday, against the status quo. And what is most inevitable about life in Russia? The cold, the constant grey clouds, the greyish-brown landscape – all of which are the perfect accompaniment to a full beard and a thick kaftan. It was this monotony that the members of Russia's first fashion subcultures were subconsciously challenging. They went far beyond the recommendations set out by Peter, whose decrees referenced German and Hungarian styles, and went straight for the chicest of them all, the French. Of course, this only applied to the aristocracy: the masses, long beards intact, observed the parade of dandies and fops from afar with a certain degree of awe.

The attire of these eighteenth-century proto-hipsters provoked exasperation, even among the educated nobility. Many writers of the time mocked them scathingly in satirical pamphlets, describing them as vapid and effeminate. Then, as now, Russia had a very fixed and very limited notion of what constitutes a 'real man'. Spending too much time on your appearance was strongly discouraged. Nowadays, that sort of thing would be described as a product of 'foreign values'. This too is nothing new. As dandyism researcher Olga Vainshtein has observed, "In the Russian mentality an interest in European fashion was directly linked with Western

Dandy and Monkey.
Ivan Bugaevsky, early
nineteenth century.
Caricature in a family album

ideology". For this reason the relationship between two of the aristocratic subcultures that are the main heroes of this chapter – the carefree dandies and the sober, revolutionary Decembrists – is entirely logical.

The eighteenth century was the golden age of the Russian nobility: a time of military victories, luxurious balls and empresses cavorting at court with handsome young rakes. The French style was all the rage, with its vividly coloured silks, satins and brocades; costumes were embroidered with glass beads, gold foil and fragments of mirrored glass. But despite this opulence, the era of the dandy had not yet come. The icon of the age was the impeccably elegant Prince Boris Kurakin, who is said never to have offended a single person in his life. But that means he was not a real dandy. A fop, a beau, a socialite maybe, but certainly not the first Russian dandy. To my mind, a true dandy wants nothing more than to offend people.

What makes a dandy really? The dandies were a movement of young aristocrats who came to the fore at the end of the eighteenth and beginning of the nineteenth century. In essence, dandyism was the first ever youth subculture. According to Russian cultural historian Yuri Lotman, "Dandyism is primarily a type of behaviour rather than a theory or ideology." (Behaviour and style, I would add.) "The basis of the dandy's behaviour is impudence and arrogance disguised by mocking civility." Thus the dual nature of dandyism emerges: on the one hand, it is a disdain for the banal, a romantic rebellion, a desire to stand out from the crowd by being a bit shocking. On the other, it means impeccable urbanity, refined clothes and manners and the confidence to insist on the superiority of your irresistible style. Perhaps it is this strange dialectic between brutality and grace which lies at the heart of the charisma of true dandies like Lord Byron and Beau Brummell.

But what of the Russian dandy? Who was he and where did he come from? Certain rakish army officers have been identified by some as the forerunners of Russian dandyism. Their uniforms were so tightly tapered at the waist, sometimes with the help of a corset, that their silhouettes rivalled the ladies. This would be matched with a high, stiff embroidered collar – a disfiguring look which was also favoured by the thoroughly unpleasant Tsar Nicholas I and which bears little resemblance to the true refinement of the dandy.

In fact, like many other subcultures, dandyism came to Russia from abroad. In the short reign of the martinet-emperor Paul I (1796-1801) the fashion excesses which characterised the gallant era of Catherine the Great were strictly forbidden. As a result, as soon as Paul's reign ended, the flamboyant French style flourished all the more. But after Russia's victory in the war against Napoleon, French excess went out of fashion and was rapidly replaced with English minimalism. So new were these fashions that national poet Alexander Pushkin had to resort to English when describing the wardrobe of the eponymous hero of his novel in verse, *Yevgeny Onegin* (1825): "But pantaloons, waistcoat, and frock, / these words are not of Russian stock". This outfit, topped with a cravat, was much sportier than the fussy frock coats that had preceded it: the dandies were the casuals of their day.

Fashionable youngsters from Moscow and St Petersburg succumbed to full-on Anglomania. They subscribed to London magazines, read Byron's *Childe Harold* and, like Brummell, spent hours in front of the mirror before venturing out. But you just can't get away from the Russianness of the Russians! Vainshtein describes the distinctive features of the Russian dandy.

The first idiosyncrasy was a passion for ostentation. Large diamonds were inserted into the silk buttons of their waistcoats and watches (preferably Breguets) were worn in pairs. Furthermore, the Russian dandies "always tried too hard, their efforts were too obvious and this immediately made them stand out… They would often feel uneasy and were afraid to make any inadvertent movements." Looking at the wealthy Russian fashionistas of the twenty-first century, you are often left with the same impression. The final, and most legitimate, difference in the style of Russian dandyism was motivated by the need for protection against the elements: "For going out in cold weather, they had coats made from thick woollen fabrics and threw an Almaviva-style cape or coat or a fur over the whole ensemble."

In addition to Vainshtein's list of Russian twists on the dandy theme, I would point out that early Russian dandyism had a distinct military bent which was not present in its European counterparts. In his biography of Brummell, Jules Barbey d'Aurevilly writes that "the dandy, who puts his own stamp of refined originality on everything (in the words of Lord Byron), cannot help but feel scornful of a uniform." The military tendency among Russian dandies was a product not of their character, but of the central role that army life played in the life of the nobility. Even Pyotr Chaadayev, the greatest dandy and free-thinker of the age, served nine years in the cavalry. The Russian military dandy resented the uniform he had to wear, but permitted himself more freedom in other areas: he used powder and blusher and wore corsets, shoulder pads and earrings. The cavalry were particularly renowned for their earrings.

Dandyism was everywhere in the Russian capital in the 1820s and 1830s. This is how Nikolai Gogol described people promenading along the streets of St Petersburg in his story *Nevsky Prospect*:

"Good heavens, what strange characters are met on the Nevsky Prospect! … In this blessed period between two and three o'clock in the afternoon, which might be called the moving centre of the Nevsky Prospect, there is a display of all the finest products of the wit of man. One exhibits a smart overcoat with the best beaver on it, the second – a lovely Greek nose, the third – superb whiskers, the fourth – a pair of pretty eyes and a marvellous hat, the fifth – a signet ring on a jaunty forefinger, the sixth – a foot in a bewitching shoe, the seventh – a cravat that excites wonder, the eighth – a moustache that reduces one to stupefaction."

Why are dandies important in Russian history? There are two reasons: one is about people, the other about influence. Two crucial figures, both already mentioned, were dandies – the scruffy but loveable poet Pushkin and the impeccably dressed philosopher Chaadayev. But its legacy goes beyond these impressive adherents: dandyism had an incredibly powerful and lasting influence as an alternative to the perennial Russian melancholy. Many of the subcultures in this book, from the futurists to hipsters via the new wave, share the dandies' devotion to exquisite audacity and immaculately dressed irony.

Although dandyism never died in Russia, its nineteenth-century heyday was short-lived. It was unable to transcend its social context: as Lotman says of the dual nature of dandyism, "While it is inseparable from individualism it simultaneously finds itself constantly dependent on its audience and therefore forever oscillates between claiming to be rebellious and coming to various compromises with society." After the defeat of the conspiracy of intermittently dandyish conspirators the Decembrists – who we will be turning to shortly – and the accession to the throne of Nicholas I in 1825, the atmosphere in the country gradually deteriorated. Pushkin, who once dreamed of assassinating the tsar, slowly turned into a court poet; Chaadayev was declared insane and imprisoned. Dandyism now eked out its existence as little more than dressing up. Some ageing Anglophiles probably still sauntered along Nevsky Prospect and peered through lorgnettes at balls, but dandyism as a movement faded along with their youth.

Decembrists

While the story of the Decembrists is both serious and tragic, you could perhaps think of it as the continuation of radical dandyism by political means. Outside of Russia, few people have heard of them, their indie band namesakes The Decembrists notwithstanding. But I really love the Decembrists. The Russian ones. For some reason I think about them a lot. I sometimes imagine how different Russia's history would have been had they succeeded in their doomed and shambolic uprising of December 1825, when a secret society made up of a handful of ex-officers tried to turn autocratic Romanov Russia into a constitutional democracy. I certainly think things would have worked out for the better. I also catch myself thinking that I would have liked to have been a Decembrist myself. Even though they failed, their revolution dissipating before it even started, the ringleaders executed or exiled.

When people talk about the Decembrists, they often mention their aristocratic descent, their education, their innate sense of nobility. But people rarely remember how very young they were. Few of the Decembrists were over 30. The five most active participants, who were all executed

PYOTR CHAADAYEV
(1794–1856)

If it was Alexander Pushkin who set the agenda for literary life in the early 19th century, it was the dandyish Pyotr Chaadayev who did the same in philosophy. A convinced European – even eventually converting to Catholicism – he despised the 'barbaric' elements of the Russian character and wasn't shy about saying so. At first this was seen as fashionable youthful rebellion, but later led conservative high society to label him a madman and shun him.

Self-portraits.
Alexander Pushkin, 1820s

for their role in the conspiracy, were Mikhail Bestuzhev-Ryumin (24 years old), Pyotr Kakhovsky (26), Sergei Muraviev-Apostol (29), Pavel Pestel (32) and Kondraty Ryleev (30). Never in the history of Russia have such young people been so ambitious in the goals of their resistance. In contrast, by 1917 the Bolsheviks were already pretty grizzled and balding. Looking back on this from our own perpetually immature twenty-first century, it seems absolutely incredible. And the Decembrists were conscious of their youth too, frequently talking about 'our generation' in their speeches and poetry. Dmitry Zavalishin, a young naval officer at the time of the revolt, wrote: "Our so-called superiors were either non-entities or dishonest – something which was all the more obvious when you compare them to our generation, who were gifted, educated and had absolute integrity."

The story of the Decembrists can be divided into three periods. The first is the gradual creation of a secret society and the decade of preparation for the uprising. The second is the unsuccessful uprising itself in St Petersburg, which lasted all of one day – 14 December 1825. The third period encapsulates all the consequences of that day – their trial,

Silhouettes of the five executed Decembrists: Pavel Pestel, Mikhail Bestuzhev-Ryumin, Pyotr Kakhovsky, Sergei Muraviev-Apostol and Kondraty Ryleev. Medallion on the cover page of Alexander Herzen and Nikolai Ogarev's almanac Polar Star. 1st January 1855

sentencing and punishment. This period dragged on almost until the end of the nineteenth century when the last of those who had taken a stand died of old age. I would describe the first period as chaotic and romantic. The second was a total disaster. The third was picturesque but tragic. The Decembrists were, without doubt, beautiful and noble. But what was the end result of all this hard work and moral purity? They were basically a group of hopeless failures who ruined their own lives and those of thousands of soldiers loyal to them. Their whole programme had become obsolete within twenty years. And, according to the astute Chaadayev, their revolt set the country back fifty years.

Yet still, when we look back on them, our eyes well up with tears of admiration. Where did the Decembrists come from? As one of them, Ivan Muraviev-Apostol, put it, "We were the children of 1812". That was the year in which Napoleon's 600,000-strong Grande Armée invaded Russia, took

Moscow, and then, over the course of a long winter campaign, was driven from the country and pursued all the way to Paris. This conflict, which came to be known as the Patriotic War, was a great shock to the country and caused the winds of change to blow throughout Russia. Exiled dissident Alexander Herzen was correct when he said:

"The period between 1810 and 1820 is not long, but 1812 comes in between these two dates… The morals are the same, the spirit is the same, the landowners returning to the burnt capital from their villages are the same. But something has changed. An idea was brought from abroad into the country, and whoever it touched with its breath became something which they had not been before."

The most profound changes took place within the army. For the first time many officers, having bonded with common soldiers on the field of battle and in everyday life, felt affected by the plight of the ordinary people. During his trial, the Decembrist Alexander Bestuzhev wrote to the tsar from prison:

"The war was still going on when the rank-and-file soldiers, returning home, were the first to spread murmurs of discontent among the people. We have spilt our own blood for you, they said, and yet we are still forced to sweat as serfs. We have saved our motherland from a tyrant and yet we find ourselves again tyrannised by the gentry."

Ruled by the 'tyrant' Napoleon it may have been, but Europe as a whole, and France in particular, were much freer than Russia, where peasants were still serfs, legally the possessions of landowners, and where even the idea of a constitution was seen as sedition. But the virus of free-thinking had infected a significant proportion of the officer corps. In 1822 a French diplomat reported on the rising tide of liberalism: "Madness and insanity has reached such a pitch among the Guards that one general recently told us that the only reason there isn't a mutiny is because there is no-one to lead them… Fifty officers were at a meeting and so excited were they by the heated and intemperate arguments about political events that they closed the meeting by rising from the table, passing in a line in front of a portrait of the emperor and taking it in turns to curse at him."

Execution of the Decembrists.
Alexander Pushkin, 1826

It is unlikely that a meeting such as the one described above would have taken place in the barracks, but young conspirators, who really did exist, had plenty of cosy places to meet. These conspiratorial meetings led to the creation of clandestine organisations such as the Union of Salvation and the Union of Welfare, which in turn fed into the two secret societies the Decembrist rebels came from, the Northern Society in St Petersburg and the Southern Society in Ukraine.

Many of the Decembrists, including one of the leaders of the Southern Society, Pavel Pestel, were also members of Masonic lodges, which has inspired some to suggest that the entire movement was the fruit of some Masonic conspiracy – a hypothesis that does not stand up to scrutiny. The most popular places, however, for free-thinkers to gather together were

scandalous poetry clubs like the Green Lamp, Arzamas and The society of Loud Laughter. In fact the Green Lamp has been seen as something like the literary wing of the Union of Welfare. Now that's somewhere I'd like to have gone. Pushkin was a regular visitor and, years after the failed uprising, he described the so-called 'orgies' held there in *Yevgeny Onegin*:

> At first these conversations
> Between Clicquot and Lafitte,
> Were friendly disputes
> And the science of rebellion,
> Did not go deep into their hearts.
> It was simply boredom,
> The idleness of young minds,
> Of grown-up rogues at play.

The topic 'Pushkin and the Decembrists' is standard fare in Russian schools. Pushkin was of the same generation as many of the rebels and he was firm friends with half a dozen or so prominent Decembrists. His closest friend, Ivan Pushchin, who was sent into exile, told the poet about the existence of the secret society, although he did not insist that Pushkin should join. As he often said later, "How could I do that when it would have meant he might face the scaffold?" There is an odd and apocryphal story about what happened to Pushkin on the eve of the uprising. He is said to have left his family estate in the morning in order to join his friends in St Petersburg that evening. Had he made that journey he would most definitely have been in lead conspirator Kondraty Ryleev's apartment on the Moika river that night, where a 'hornet's nest' of Decembrist conspirators gathered until the early hours discussing the details of the coup. He would have joined them on Senate Square, and possibly in Siberia too, or on the gallows. Luckily, this did not come to pass. While Pushkin was driving up the avenue leading from his manor house, a hare suddenly jumped across

Nobody Gives a Fuck About Pestel: Commemoration of the Decembrists.
Voina, 2008. Courtesy of Alexei Plutser-Sarno

Voina is a revolutionary art group that engages in radical street protest actions. More than twenty criminal cases have been brought against the group. Voina activists have experienced dozens of arrests, searches, as sault sand batteries committed by Russian cops. Activists Leonid Nikolaev and Oleg Vorotnikov were detained in jail, accused of inciting hatred towards the police with their art. They were released from custody when Banksy bailed them out. The *Guardian* wrote about Voina: "Banksy is donating all royalties to the Voina artist co-operative in Russia, two of whom are currently residing in a St Petersburg jail... Alexei Plutser-Sarno, Voina's chief ideologue, told the *Guardian* that Banksy had contacted the group after hearing about the imprisoned pair. We're very grateful for his support, he said. Banksy's help will attract the attention of the whole world to the personal repression aimed at us, as well as to the greater problem of liquidation of democracy in Russia." At the present moment members of the Voina Group are wanted by the Russian police and Interpol.

Alexei Plutser-Sarno

the road in front of the carriage and the superstitious poet told the driver to turn around. He stayed at home that night.

While there are doubts around the veracity of this legend, it is easy to see why it is so popular: Russians can live with Pushkin being superstitious, but never a coward or a hypocrite. However, as one can see from later events, Pushkin's absence from the square was perhaps not entirely the result of a stroke of luck. Soon after the uprising, he wrote a conciliatory letter to Nicholas I and in early September the new tsar not only recalled him from exile, but also became his personal censor. Pushkin continued to be slightly disrespectful to the tsar, but in general, when Nicholas told his court "Now he is mine!", he was right. Like a true dandy, Pushkin chose a sensible compromise.

If Pushkin had decided to become a Decembrist, it is not entirely clear what he would have been signing up for. Their programme was not particularly harmonious or uniform. The Southern Society was considered to be more radical: its agenda was dictated by its leader Pestel's inflammatory manifesto, *Russian Truth*, in which he called for Russia to become a republic governed by a people's assembly, with mass land redistribution and equal rights for all classes. The Northern Society also insisted on the abolition of slavery and the legal protection of civil rights, but proposed a constitutional monarchy with a parliament, on the British model; the peasants would be freed, but not own their land.

In the end, when the uprising took place unexpectedly in December 1825, neither plan was used. The rebellion had been intended for the summer of 1826, but the unexpected death of Alexander I on 19 November and the vague wording of the abdication of his brother Prince Constantine gave the would-be revolutionaries hope that a swift, improvised intervention backed by the military could prevent the coronation of Alexander's unpopular brother Nicholas.

The political programme for this uprising was a hastily drawn up 'Manifesto to the Russian People', which granted all power to an interim government headed by a temporary 'dictator', Prince Sergei Trubetskoy. The day of the uprising itself, 14 December, was a tragic fiasco. The would-be dictator Trubetskoy took fright and went to hide at the house of the Austrian ambassador, a relative of his. Another rebel, Pyotr Kakhovsky, who was supposed to assassinate the tsar, instead shot the military commander of St Petersburg, Mikhail Miloradovich. Captain Yakubovich refused to storm the Winter Palace or to arrest the tsar's family; Colonel Bulatov failed to seize the Peter and Paul Fortress. The manifesto was left blowing in the wind and 4,500 soldiers and rebel officers spent all day standing stock still on the square in the freezing cold, until at dusk they were fired upon by cannons at close range. I can't understand why they just stood there, a massive, immobile target, even though the Winter Palace was only a few hundred metres away. But ours is not to reason why.

Drawing from the series
Black Portraits. Victoria
Lomasko, 2011–13.
Courtesy of the artist

A woman recites Alexander Pushkin's
Ode to Liberty in the metro:

And silent stands the faithless guard
The drawbridge downed without alarm
The gate in dark of night unbarred
By treason's mercenary arm.
O shame! O terror of our time!
Those Janissary beasts burst in And slash
The Criminal Sovereign
Is slaughtered by unholy crime.

"Pushkin is our great poet.
Everything else is tawdry."

The following day all of the organisers of the uprising were arrested. In the south a mutiny by the Chernigov Regiment was also quickly cut short. The five ringleaders were hanged, 120 conspirators were sentenced to a life of hard labour in Siberia, and hundreds of officers were demoted to the ranks and sent as cannon fodder to the war in the Caucasus. Siberia marked the beginning of an epic new chapter in the story of the Decembrists. In areas that are still now remote like Yakutia, Irkutsk and Lake Baikal they worked in the mines, shackled and under close supervision. As a contribution to the history of their beloved fatherland, their hopeless, confused uprising pales in comparison with their considerable role in the development of Siberia. But the most romantic and heroic aspect of this whole tale – and the theme of countless books and films – concerns not the Decembrists, but their wives. Eleven angel-faced young noble ladies followed their convict husbands into exile. Recalling the experience, Pauline Gueble, the French wife of exile Ivan Annenkov, said: "I must admit that there was much that was poetic in our lives." This is reiterated by Pushkin's friend Pushchin: "The most important thing is not to lose the poetry of life; it remains with me to this day." This is the real gift that these failed rebels gave Russia – not a new constitution, but a new way of being. Yuri Lotman put it this way: "The Decembrists showed great creative energy in forming a particular type of Russian person whose behaviour is very different to anything which came before it in Russian history." He describes the basic qualities of this new type as follows:

- The Decembrist is a man of action, focused on practical changes in the political life in Russia
- Paradoxically, his main form of action is verbal
- The Decembrist cultivates seriousness as normal behaviour
- The Decembrist always believes that he is playing a role on an important historical stage
- The Decembrist always speaks out. The Decembrist publicly calls a spade a spade
- The Decembrist is chivalrous. This is what makes him so ethical, but it is also what it makes him vulnerable in the face of general turpitude
- The Decembrist is required to behave heroically
- The Decembrist respects the cult of brotherhood
- Political organisations are based on intimacy, not just shared beliefs
- As aristocratic revolutionaries, the Decembrist adheres to a well-established code of honour

The Decembrists, with their passion for the 'poetry of life', with their ideal of behaviour to which they remained loyal to the end, created a moral code for all progressive Russians that succeeded them. There were many revolutionaries in Russia after the Decembrists: Populists, Socialist Revolutionaries, Marxists and Anarchists, but none of them came close to the nobility, humanity and self-sacrifice of these aristocratic predecessors. Just before he appeared on Senate Square, the poet and Decembrist Kondraty Ryleev, later executed, wrote:

> I know that death awaits
> Whoever is the first to rebel
> Against the oppressors of the people.
> My fate is already certain
> But where, tell me, has freedom
> Ever been won without sacrifice?

One hundred and ninety years have passed since then. There is still no freedom in Russia. And, although their memory lives on, there are no Decembrists either.

Superfluous Men

The Decembrists had a noble cause, but they did not have a particular style that set them apart. The dandies had a look, but no cause to speak of. The aristocratic subculture that followed them, the so-called superfluous men, had neither a style nor a cause. Worse still, they didn't even know that they were superfluous men. Perhaps if they had known, if they had thought of themselves as a community, then their unnecessary lives might have turned out differently. But no, every one of them searched for a meaning to life on his own, and usually failed to find it. So who were these superfluous men? The Decembrists and the dandies existed in real life. We have their letters, their portraits and their memoirs. But the term "superfluous man" was first coined by the novelist Ivan Turgenev and all the canonical examples are fictional characters.

Turgenev noticed that, after the failure of the Decembrists, Russian literature came to be populated by heroes who, while bright and well meaning, could find no satisfaction in life and lacked the will to change anything. Avatars of the superfluous man include the delicate and sensitive Onegin, the intelligent and critical Alexander Chatsky from Alexander Griboyedov's satirical play *Woe from Wit* (1825) and the dashing Grigory Pechorin from Mikhail Lermontov's *A Hero of Our Time* (1840). It's not for nothing, however, that classic Russian literature is renowned for its realism: the superfluous men were drawn from life. The superfluous men were no fools: they were well educated, good looking and not necessarily lazy per se – so what was it that made them surplus to requirements? Well, in the first place, they were honest and conscientious and did not tolerate unscrupulousness. Tolstoy describes a similar trait in his favourite character in *War and Peace* (1869), Pierre Bezukhov:

**MIKHAIL LERMONTOV
(1814–1841)**

The Jim Morrison of nineteenth-century Russian literature – bold, defiant, tragic and dead in his late twenties – Lermontov has always been the poet of choice for gloomy Russian teens. Upbeat patriots cannot bear the thought that this great poet was the author of a viciously satirical poem beginning "Farewell, unwashed Russia, land of slaves and land of masters." Even more significant than his verse, however, is his sole novel, *A Hero of Our Time*, an embittered tale of misanthropic romanticism.

The Aristocrat's Breakfast. Pavel Fedotov, 1849–50. Courtesy of the State Tretyakov Gallery, Moscow

Pierre at the Battle of Borodino.
Dmitry Shmarinov, 1953.
Illustration to *War and Peace*

"He had the unfortunate capacity that many men, especially Russians, have of seeing and believing in the possibility of goodness and truth, but of seeing the evil and falsehood of life too clearly to be able to take a serious part in it. Every sphere of work was connected, in his eyes, with evil and deception. Whatever he tried to be, whatever he engaged in, the evil and falsehood of it repulsed him and blocked every path of activity."

Many of my friends would recognise themselves in this description; to some extent I do too.

The second reason for this superfluity is that this generation, in their individual characteristics and in their position in society, did not seem to fit in with the times in which they lived. They were born either too early or too late, or in the wrong place. Chatsky returns from studying in civilised Europe and immediately finds himself stifled by the philistine company of his compatriots; by the end of the play, he is promising never to return to Moscow again. Pechorin, Lermontov's dissolute adventurer in the Caucasus, is born too late: 15 years younger and he would have made an exemplary hero in the Napoleonic wars or a perfect Decembrist. Instead he ends up as an example of the contradiction between "a profound character and an empty life", as the critic Vissarion Belinsky put it. He is guided by a principle of 'search and destroy' – stealing horses, breaking hearts and killing off friendships, sometimes quite literally – but all this gets him nowhere.

Of the classic literary triumvirate, *Yevgeny Onegin* is the least convincing. That said, maybe it's this vagueness that makes him so memorable. Pushkin goes on about this handsome fellow for eight chapters, only to have his would-be "London dandy" be shown the door by a principled Russian girl, Tatiana. All superfluous men, throughout the ages, have been extremely unlucky in love. If they fall in love then it is unrequited; if someone falls in love with them, the consequences are dire.

While characters like Onegin were initially viewed with hostility, by the 1840s and 1850s political stagnation had made the whole country

*Oblomov on the Sofa.*1954.
Tatyana Shishmareva.
Illustration to *Oblomov*

bored and frustrated, just like the superfluous men. Herzen said: "We are all in some sense Onegins, if only in the fact that we would prefer to be him than some bureaucrat or landowner." It reminds me of the situation in the USSR from the mid-Sixties to the mid-Eighties: life was relatively stable and tediously prosperous. Back then this overwhelming boredom helped cause the phenomenon known as 'internal emigration', when hundreds of thousands of Soviet superfluous men and women mentally disappeared off into their own little worlds. In the nineteenth century this problem didn't exist: normal, 'external' emigration was possible and many took this option. Chatsky led the way, and he was followed by many other superfluous men, such as the eponymous hero of Turgenev's own *Rudin* (1856), who, unlike many of his colleagues, eventually roused himself to action and perished on the barricades in Paris during the 1848 Revolution.

Rudin's heroic death raises a question first formulated back in 1840 by Belinsky, who wondered why, when Russia is "dominated by malefactors and mediocrities, where everything that is noble and gifted stagnates in shameful inactivity," is it only the Europeans, who "when they are suffering, throw themselves into political activity and through that find an escape from their suffering?" One might continue his thought: Must Russians forever drown their suffering in gloom and self-destruction? We're still looking for an answer to that question.

By the early 1860s the gallery of literary superfluous men was almost full. In real life they were not decreasing in numbers, although they were no longer young. Worse still, their role in society, which during the reign of Nicholas I was, if not progressive, then at least neutral, had become decidedly reactionary after Nicholas's successor Alexander II came to the throne in 1856, determined to bring about reform. The superfluous men were nobles who did not want to serve a state which they found repulsive and did not want to exploit their peasant serfs actively. For that you've got to hand it to them. But they either refused or were unable find a place in the nascent capitalist system and make their own way in business, finance, industry or anything else that they preferred to dismiss as unsuitable for aristocrats. They were victims of a decaying monarchy and of the system of serfdom, but they were also parasites on those very institutions. By the 1860s, criticism of the already unhappy superfluous men had become an everyday occurrence, with satirists like Mikhail Saltykov-Shchedrin skewering their indolence and conservatism. The idle Russian nobles turned into a grumbling and miserable appendix to society – although not without a certain Chekhovian charm. And this is where the superfluous men of the nineteenth century came to an end. That said, Russian life always gives you a chance to be superfluous! Almost every generation in this country could be considered a 'lost generation'. But this instinct for idleness is also a problem, as much a cause of Russia's problems as its instinct for ideologues.

Slavophiles and Zapadniki

All the fundamental events of the twentieth century had their roots in the subcultures of the nineteenth. The Decembrists provided the impetus and moral model for the revolutionary movement. The dandies infected society with the viral predilection for an alternative style that has kept spawning new trends up to the present day. The superfluous man led to the creation of a new type of Russian – the internal emigrant. And it was in the era of the superfluous men, the 1830s and 1840s, that we saw the first clear formulation of a crucial ideological debate which still rages to this day: where does Russia belong? Is it a European country like all the others, or is it fundamentally different?

Caricature of Ivan Aksakov.
Petr Kurenkov, 1867.
Journal Budilnik

In Russia's more recent history, the unceasing struggle between globalism and nationalism has periodically taken a brutal and sometimes bloody turn. For example, the Bolshevik revolution was of a decidedly internationalist character, while the Stalinist 'struggle against cosmopolitism' was chauvinistic and anti-Semitic; Gorbachev's reforms pulled the country into a European and global orbit, but Putin's superstition and so-called patriotism have again isolated Russia.

But it all began much more gently. From the 1850s, the two camps in this debate have been known as the Slavophiles and the *zapadniki*, or *westernisers*. Both recognised that Russia had specific problems, like the continued existence of serfdom, but while the latter sought European solutions to them, the former thought only homegrown remedies were applicable (hence the notion that they 'loved the slavs'). The nobility were the dominant force both among the *zapadniki* and the Slavophiles but, importantly, a very active role was for the first time played by individuals from lower social classes, like the *zapadnik* Vissarion Belinsky, the son of a doctor, and the Slavophile industrialist Fyodor Chizhov. Members of both

Do Russians want war? From the series *Russian Questions*. Vladislav Mamyshev-Monroe, 1997.
Collection of Vladimir Ovcharenko

Marfusha. From the series *Russian Questions*. Vladislav Mamyshev-Monroe, 1997.
Collection of Vladimir Ovcharenko

camps moved in the same social circles and many of them were linked, if not by close friendships, then by affectionate respect. After heated arguments in meetings and clubs they would walk with their arms around each other to the drinking house.

Their debates went beyond theory and also posed some concrete, practical questions, with lasting implications: should we develop industry or agriculture? Is capitalism a force for good or evil for Russia? What is more suitable for the country: wage labour or voluntary communal work? The questions arising from the choice between East and West also included subcultural issues of how to dress and how to behave.

It is a paradox that the two opposing solutions to the question of Russia's place in the world were both inspired by the Patriotic War of 1812–1814. The *zapadniki* became aware of the progressive elements of Europe and the freedom that was blossoming there and the patriotic Slavophiles gloried in Russia's role in guaranteeing these freedoms by force of arms. Personally, I can see that it is always more exciting to believe that your country is exceptional and that what it has achieved is unique. On an emotional level, therefore, I understand the Slavophiles and their defence of Russia's originality and singularity. The *zapadnik* attitude was actually much duller. For them Russia was just lagging behind the civilised world by about fifty years, and needed only to follow the path that England and France had already trodden. One of the founders of this tendency, Chaadayev, characterised life in Russia in his day as a gloomy existence, devoid of strength and energy, enlivened only by crime and softened only by serfdom. There are no captivating recollections or gracious images in the memory of the Russian people, nor are there any useful lessons from its past. We live only within the cramped constraints of the present, without a past or a future, in a state of lifeless stagnation. Chaadayev identified the Russian Orthodox Church as one of the main reasons for Russia's backwardness, which he saw as overly materialistic and as inspiring nothing but torpor. Orthodoxy was a major sticking point between the Slavophiles and the *zapadniki*.

Leading Slavophiles saw Orthodoxy as the core of Russianness and in 1834 conservative statesman Count Sergei Uvarov coined a three-word slogan for Russian nationalist ideology: "Orthodoxy, Autocracy, Nationalism" (the antithesis of "Liberté, Egalité, Fraternité"). Armed with Orthodoxy, the Slavophiles intended to teach the decadent West a lesson by leaving it behind, along with its empty values and atheism. You only have to add a bit of homophobia to the mix and you can see that the recipe for patriotic rhetoric in Russia hasn't changed much in the last one hundred and fifty years. As far as autocracy was concerned, there were many differences of opinion: the *zapadniki* wavered between wanting a constitutional monarchy and a republic, and the Slavophiles were in favour of an autocratic tsar. Slavophile poet and philosopher Konstantin Aksakov argued that the Russian people were in general 'non-governmental'

"The West wants to destroy the bold and beautiful Russian people."

Stonemason Sergei, once a militant atheist, is now an Orthodox activist.

"Russians are shit. But me, I'm seventh-generation intelligentsia."

Viktor Mizin is a lecturer in political science at MGIMO, the Moscow State Institute of International Relations. He was born at Grauerman Maternity Hospital in central Moscow.

Drawing from the series *Black Portraits*. Victoria Lomasko, 2011–13.
Courtesy of the artist

by nature and that he himself had no interest in taking any kind of responsibility for the running of the country. His followers echoed this sentiment, claiming that for centuries the Russian people had co-existed with their rulers in accordance with a sort of principle of non-interference with each other, and that everything was fine until Peter the Great came on the scene with his German clothes and European values and spoiled it all. Many *zapadniki* agreed that Peter had been a cruel despot, but they also idolised him for setting Russia on the road to civilisation.

The importance of the East versus West debate is as evident as its futility. But how does it fit into our subcultural story? Both the Slavophiles and the *zapadniki* were intellectual movements that had no organised structure as such and no clear leaders. But they did both have an aesthetic ideal, particularly the Slavophiles. Aksakov's first appearance in high society caused a scandal because of his chosen outfit of boots, a red shirt and a traditional *murmolka* fur hat. This look was inspired by a precise underlying ideology: "It's time we grew closer to our own people and for this we must cast off those ridiculous short-cut German clothes which keep us apart from them," he once said. And then he bowed to the ground, picked up the frock coat he had cast off, and threw it contemptuously aside saying: "Peter tore us from our national heritage and forced us to shave our beards. We must now grow them back and return to our heritage." He then turned to one of the great society beauties of the day and said: "Cast off your German dress! Why go on the hunt for men with that? Set an example to our ladies and wear a *sarafan* (a traditional Russian peasant dress). See how it suits your beautiful face!"

What is more, these were real youth movements. At the time of the supposed formation of the core Slavophile group in 1839 our friend Aksakov was 22 years old, while his ally and younger brother Ivan was 16. Even their older comrade, the poet Alexei Khomyakov, was only 35. The *zapadniki* group formed at around the same time, catalysed by the publication in 1836 of Chaadayev's *Philosophical Letters*, a sort of manifesto for 'Europeanism' in Russia. Their first meetings in 1840 were attended by some young men already familiar to us, such as Alexander Herzen (28), Vissarion Belinsky (29) and Ivan Turgenev (22). Chaadayev himself had turned 46.

It seems to me that practically all subcultures and youth movements in Russia adopt either a 'Western' or a 'Russian' feel. As well as the obvious things, such as a love for foreign music or nationalist politics, the differences between the two camps can have more nuanced characteristics. It's commonly accepted that latter-day *zapadniki* pay much more attention to their physical appearance, are more reserved and neat, display a penchant for criticism and irony, prefer small groups to rowdy crowds, and are inclined to experiments and novelty. For their part, the Slavophiles' anti-Western descendants tend to be more open and soulful, although often also aggressive, sentimental and conservative. In other words, it's not just a matter of taste and political views, but also of a particular mentality. Perhaps this is why supposedly superficial matters of 'stylistic' disagreement between different subcultures are constantly evolving into all-consuming hatreds. This has become especially apparent in Russia over the last few decades. We have come a long way from the friendly disagreements of the originators of this schism in Russian life, the *zapadniki* and the Slavophiles, who were at least united, as Herzen wrote, by their "unaccountable, physical, passionate love for the Russian people".

By the 1850s, however, the passionate arguments had lost their fervour and those involved had grown older; some of them had moved on (Chaadayev) and others had emigrated (Herzen and Bakunin).

As with the superfluous men, the reforms of Alexander II made their concerns seem anachronistic, in part by fulfilling some of the demands of both the *zapadniki* and the Slavophiles, such as the freeing of the serfs. A whole era gradually sunk into oblivion together with these sweet people, the likes of whom we will never see again: the age of aristocratic protest. It was an era of beautiful, empty thoughts, of appeals to reason. A time of noble, courageous gestures which were sadly useless, despite having been made with a vaguely refined and naïve charm which has never been seen since in Russian dissident culture.

Nevertheless, the aristocratic subcultures of the first half of the nineteenth century have a rich inheritance in the history of Russian resistance: the dandies introduced a European lightness and independence; the Decembrists shared their love of freedom; the Slavophiles and *zapadniki* posed the central question of Russia's place in the world; the superfluous men proved that the aristocracy was finished as a force for change. Its privileges had left it devoid of vitality: coddled aristocrats were sickened by any sign of initiative and the entrepreneurial spirit that came naturally to merchants and to the new bourgeoisie. Even the lack of money among the newly poor representatives of the upper classes could not force them into work. Instead they would scrounge off friends and relatives, sit in wait for an inheritance or sell off the wealth of their ancestors. The nobles' former trump card, a good education, no longer provided the advantages it once had and often led to little more than lazy philosophising. Meanwhile, there was growing pressure on them from a new generation that was rude, badly dressed and incredibly ambitious. A generation which brought a dash of dynamism to the vast, slow Russian empire.

Student-Nihilist. Ilya Repin, 1883. Courtesy of the Far Eastern Art Museum, Khabarovsk, Russia

CHAPTER 2

The Real Deal: Raznochintsy and Nihilists. 1861–1870

There is no real equivalent in English for the Russian word *raznochintsy*. It is important, however, to explain its meaning and to do so we must take a short excursion through the intricate landscape of the Russian class system in the middle of the nineteenth century. There were five basic classes: the nobility, the clergy, the merchant class, the petite bourgeoisie and the peasantry. Each class had its own laws, privileges and limitations. The nobility, the petty bourgeoisie and the peasantry were all hereditary classes, with status passed on from generation to generation. Being a member of the clergy or the merchant class was determined not by birth but by profession.

Inevitably, and with increasing frequency as time went on, people appeared who did not fit into these categories. There were various ways in which individuals slipped into the cracks between the classes: there were the illegitimate children of the nobility, merchants who had lost their fortunes, the children of priests and military personnel from a 'common' background. Most importantly there were young people who moved into a different class by attending university. All of these people came to be known as *raznochintsy*. Many of the *zapadniki* were also *raznochintsy*, like Belinsky, who was descended from a long line of priests. Perceptive French traveller the Marquis de Custine had singled out the sons of clergymen as a particularly dynamic force as early as the 1830s: "I have not yet mentioned one class whose representatives are neither members of the nobility nor commoners and this is the sons of priests. Most of them get churned out into the army of government officials – the veritable plague of Russia. These gentlemen are something like 'second-rate' nobles and yet are extremely hostile to the nobility. They are imbued with an anti-aristocratic fervour but at the same time are happy with the oppression of serfs. I am sure that it is this element that will spark a revolution in Russia."

The evolution of capitalism created demand for white collar workers – not necessarily just government officials but professionals too. One of the first and most important reforms instigated by Alexander II in the 1860s was to remove restrictions preventing 'the underprivileged

**NIKOLAI CHERNYSHEVSKY
(1828–1889)**

Relatively unknown in the West but, quite possibly, nineteenth-century Russia's most influential left-wing thinker and writer. Chernyshevsky's active life and work ended at the age of 35 when he was sentenced to hard labour and exile in Siberia, but a decade of work before then was enough to inspire several generations of Russian revolutionary democrats and socialists.

What Is To Be Done?
Nikolai Chernyshevsky.
Cover of 1867 edition

classes' from receiving an education and to increase the number of free places for poor students in educational establishments. Young people now rushed to universities – and emerged from them as *raznochintsy*. It would be an exaggeration, however, to say that all the *raznochintsy* were highly educated.

Nevertheless, there is no doubt that the famous Russian intelligentsia emerged, to a significant extent, from the ranks of the *raznochintsy*. But the two are far from equivalent. Nor does the Russian concept of intelligentsia fully correlate with the term 'intellectual'. The meaning of the intellectual is fairly prosaic: a highly educated person who performs intellectual labour. A member of the intelligentsia – an *intelligent* in Russian, with a hard 'g' – is also well educated but this is only a necessary, not a sufficient, criterion for gaining admission to this group. Alongside academic knowledge and professional skills, an intelligent must adhere to a clear moral and ethical code of conduct. For those in the intelligentsia, be they right-leaning liberals or leftist socialists, the agenda must always include honesty, empathy for others and some personal involvement with the country's problems. It is this preoccupation with morality which distinguishes them from clever but heartless 'intellectuals'.

I should note that the authorities in Russia have, as a rule, always hated the intelligentsia, whether openly or not, seeing in it a loud and un-pleasant, if not fatal, enemy to its governmental successes. The tsars con-sidered the intelligentsia a hotbed of revolt and unrest; in a fit of anger, Lenin, who was himself a certified intellectual, once called it the "shit of the nation"; Stalin methodically destroyed it; Putin is forcing it into emigration. Perhaps only Gorbachev, and to a certain extent Yeltsin, sensed that this conscientious section of society could serve as their power base.

Despite their undoubted idealism, the qualities that define the intel-ligentsia owe much to the *raznochintsy* and their ineradicable vigour for the national wellbeing. The *raznochintsy* were a varied collection of peo-ple. Only two factors united them: first, they did not belong to a particular class and, second, they had some sort of education. So we come to the logical question: can you really consider the *raznochintsy* a subculture?

They certainly had distinctive features. They were far more energetic and enterprising than the young nobles of their time and were practically unanimous in being disillusioned with the government, the aristocracy and the status quo in Russia. One can understand why: these unwanted children of society had had to work extra hard to find a place in the sun, if they ever did find one. But despite all their hard work, not to mention their many talents and merits, they never achieved the status that was the birth right of the nobles. The *raznochintsy* were great supporters of profound and urgent social reforms which glimmered in front of them with the Revo-lution of 1917.

The *raznochintsy* had no particular passion for culture; on the contrary, they were rather dismissive of the value of art. They were not well-off, so needed to pursue a career and had a general contempt for aristocratic 'idiocies'. The *raznochintsy* had no dress code and dandyism was totally anathema to them. However, looking at the portraits of prominent *raznochintsy*, one can see many similarities: they tended to have quite long, well-groomed hair, usually with a side parting. They wore oval or round spectacles, dark clothes and no accessories. Some notable exponents of this unremarkable look were the talented and articulate *raznochintsy* critics that took the Russian cultural world by storm in the 1860s. Soviet historians usually refer to them as 'revolutionary democrats', but I prefer the name they used for themselves: Realists. At the peak of their fame in the 1860s, the most prominent Realists were young, like the radical Dmitri Pisarev (born in 1840) and the kind and wise Nikolai Dobrolyubov (1836). But the dominant figure was Nikolai Chernyshevsky (1828). Chernyshevsky is virtually unknown outside Russia. This is a great mistake, as he is a major figure. Karl Marx learned Russian in order to read his articles (among other things). In 1853 Chernyshevsky arrived in St Petersburg from the provincial town of Saratov and wrote a sensational thesis called *The aesthetic relationship between art and reality*, arguing for the primacy of ultimate realism in art and criticising "art for art's sake". He started working as a teacher and as a journalist at the progressive literary magazine *The Contemporary*. His scientific and critical works laid the foundation for the formation of a secret society called 'Land and Freedom' (more of which later) and he is presumed to be the author of the proclamation "Greetings to the Landlords' Peasantry from their Well-Wishers" which decried the abolition of serfdom as inadequate and incited the peasants to revolt. *The Contemporary* was shut down in May 1862 after publishing a number of radical critiques of the tsar's reforms. Soon afterwards Chernyshevsky was himself arrested and sent to the notorious Peter and Paul Fortress as 'Enemy Number One of the Russian Empire'. During his one and a half years in prison, Chernyshevsky wrote copiously, but his most important work from this time was the novel *What Is To Be Done?*

Classical Russian literature has given the world many masterpieces, and you can argue forever about which one is the best. But when it comes to historical influence, this book – written in four months in a prison cell – can, without exaggeration, be considered the most important Russian book of the nineteenth century. Although as a work of pure literature it is typically not valued very highly (a mistake in my opinion), even the book's most ardent critics, such as Vladimir Nabokov, would have to concede the impact it has had on the entire history of Russia. As the anarchist Prince Pyotr Kropotkin said, "It was a kind of revelation for Russian youth of the time and became a political programme – it was a beacon for them."

The plot of *What Is To Be Done?* centres on a love triangle between Vera Rozalskaya, her nominal husband and friend Dmitry Lopukhov, and her lover Alexander Kirsanov. It was the innocence and ridiculousness of this melodramatic storyline which got the manuscript of the book past the prison censor and into the hands of the publishers. The censor was later fired for this mistake. But the love plot is not what the book is really about. One of its cryptic subtitles is 'From the Tales of the New People'. And who exactly is this 'homo novus'? All the main heroes of the book are young and flawless: they live incredibly pure lives where there is no place for lies, greed or hypocrisy, where everything in the world is just and works out to the benefit of all. Many contemporaries, and later historians, called Chernyshevsky's novel the 'Bible of the young *raznochintsy*', and this seems to hold true. The author of *What Is To Be Done?* was born in a clergy family and was without a doubt well versed in scripture and in the art of preaching. The fact that his 'newest testament' is militantly materialist and atheist does not contradict this proposition. Dostoyevsky wrote that the most zealous atheism "finds itself the closest to true faith". The novel, as is expected of a religious text, describes the lives of wonderful people (who are, in their own way, holy) and their idealised relationships. For thousands upon thousands of young *raznochintsy* of both sexes, this was the ultimate paradigm to imitate, and not just on the surface, as is often the case with subcultures: the novel had a deep shaping influence on their behaviour.

The plot of *What Is To Be Done?* is simple – as befits a textbook for real life. After escaping an unhappy childhood, Vera Pavlovna founds a commune of seamstresses where all the earnings are divided out equally. Two other couples also live in the commune – they are 'new people'. Life is built on the principle that one should be honest about one's emotions. The priority is feeling pleasure in responsibilities. There is a clear separation between love and sex. All of this is an illustration of Chernyshevsky's theory of 'rational egoism', which is a sort of mix of altruism and behavioural Darwinism: man, as part of nature, strives for personal gain and satisfaction. However, being drawn into society means his own interests become subordinate to public interests, which at the end of the day works out to be to his own advantage.

The 'new people' lead lives of crystal-clear righteousness, even among the general filth and beastliness of daily life. Foremost among them is the mysterious yogi Rakhmetov, a professional revolutionary. His image proved highly attractive to young people and especially students.

Herzen wrote: "Young Russians after 1862 almost all belonged to the *What Is To Be Done?* era." A good illustration of this is the story of Polish revolutionary Jarosław Dąbrowski (at the time Poland was part of the Russian empire). In 1864 Dąbrowski managed to escape from detention in Moscow – a strange city where he knew no-one. He went up to the first student he saw in the street with 'an honest face' and explained his situation to him. The student embraced him and uttered the now classic phrase: "Your freedom is our freedom." Then he took Dąbrowski and introduced him to his friends, who forged documents for him to get back to Poland. These were all 'new people'.

The story of the proponents of Realism ended quickly and tragically. After prison Chernyshevsky was sent into exile and stayed there, despite many efforts to secure his release. His colleagues Dobrolyubov and Pisarev died young, at 25 and 28, from illness and drowning respectively. However, their writing inspired Russia for many years to come. The 'new people' quietly faded away over the next decade but *What Is To Be Done?* continued to be revered by many staunch Russian revolutionaries, from Lenin's Bolsheviks to the Futurist Vladimir Mayakovsky, who all read it as a manual for the twentieth century.

The story of the *raznochintsy* and the ideology of *What Is To Be Done?* had one more legacy – one that was paradoxical and much mythologised but still unarguably important. In it, the ideology, lifestyle and political activity of the radical *raznochintsy* took on their definitive, and most extreme, form. On the other hand, this phenomenon turned out to be overly 'literary', much like the superfluous men, and politically poisonous. What I am talking about is nihilism, an idea which shaped the fate of Russian liberalism at the end of the 1860s and early 1870s.

The word 'nihilist' first started appearing in critical articles, especially those written by Dobrolyubov, and had different meanings and contexts, usually as a synonym for 'sceptic'. But the word acquired a new life and a new celebrity in the spring of 1862 with the publication of Ivan Turgenev's *Fathers and Sons*. The main protagonist of the novel, Yevgeny Bazarov, was the first and most important nihilist in history. Turgenev recalled that on returning to the capital in May 1862 he found St Petersburg in flames, the result of a damaging and mysterious conflagration. The first acquaintance that he met readily offered an explanation: "See what your nihilists are doing – they're burning St Petersburg!"

So who exactly were these terrible arsonists? (incidentally, rumours that buildings in St Petersburg were being set on fire by 'nihilists' or 'Poles' were never actually confirmed). The nihilists were an interesting mix of a virtual and a real-life subculture, with more of the real than the literary. The nihilists had one thing in common with the superfluous men, and that was that their name had been created by a writer – indeed by the same one. Both names are fairly pejorative: it's unlikely that many of the superfluous men would actually consider themselves to be superfluous.

In the same way, the nihilists rarely called themselves that, preferring their self-description as 'thinking Realists', 'the progressive youth' or simply 'the new people'. When it comes down to it, they were the young people from *What Is To Be Done?*, just slightly less idealistic.

In Turgenev's novel Bazarov's friend, Arkady Kirsanov, himself an aspiring (and soon to be disillusioned) nihilist describes their world-view as follows: "A nihilist is a man who does not bow down before any authority, who does not take any principle on faith, whatever reverence that principle may be enshrined in." It is important to realise that the word 'principles' here means not just archaic, feudal-monarchic dogmas but also liberal

**IVAN TURGENEV
(1818–1883)**

"A wonderful, but not particularly profound" person according to Tolstoy, Turgenev was one one of the most fashionable writers of his time – not just in Russia, but in his beloved Europe too. Although his moderate liberalism led to a few problems with the censors, the rich nobleman Turgenev, with his fondness for hunting and the theatre, was a far cry from the rebels and radicals. Nevertheless, it was he who succeeded in creating the canonical literary depiction of Russian outsiders in *Fathers and Sons* and coining the popular terms 'superfluous men' and 'nihilists'.

Title page of *Fathers and Sons* by Ivan Turgenev, 1862. First edition

ones – that is where the conflict between Bazarov and the 'progressive' Kirsanov family arises. The philosophy of ultimate materialism is based on the natural sciences and presupposes both atheism and the repudiation of traditional morality. This also meant that emotions such as love were viewed as 'chemical reactions' – an experience of which of course drives our hero to mental torture after he meets the right girl. Politically speaking, the nihilists did not recognise the authority of the government and supported the dismantling of the existing structure, to be replaced by a rational system that worked for the good of the people. A report by the Third Department (the KGB of its day) in 1869 described the Russian nihilist as "combining the Western traits of being an atheist, a materialist, a revolutionary, a socialist and a communist. He is an avowed enemy of the state and the social system. He does not recognise the government."

The nihilist Bazarov, however, was more of a revolutionary than a moral philosopher, and Turgenev's portrayal of him is extremely vague and unconvincing. This resulted in unexpected approbation from the authorities. Here is an excerpt from a report from the same Third Department in 1863:

"Fathers and Sons, a work by the well-known writer Ivan Turgenev, has a beneficial effect on the minds of readers. Turgenev is one of the greatest contemporary Russian talents and has the sympathy of the educated classes. The younger generation who recently applauded him were surprised to find that in this work he brands our nascent revolutionaries as nihilists, and in doing so has shaken the doctrines of the materialists and their representatives to the core."

It is not surprising that the real 'new people' from Chernyshevsky's novel did not accept Bazarov being "one of their own" and considered him to be a caricature of the revolutionary *raznochintsy*.

But enough of the literati! The nihilists were different from the superfluous men, who lived quiet solitary lives, never forming a community of interests. By contrast, the nihilists came together to take an active role in the cultural, subcultural, social and, in years to come, political life of Russia.

Their moral code and lifestyle were fairly strict. The following is an extract from the diary of a St Petersburg student which was scrutinised as part of an investigation into an assassination attempt on the tsar. In it he lists the necessary qualities of a revolutionary materialist:

ABSTINENCE: do not eat fit to burst, don't drink yourself under the table.
SILENCE: speak only of that which is useful to yourself and others.
ORDERLINESS: everything must have its specific place.
Set aside an hour of your time for each task.
RESOLVE: decide what you must do and do it.
MODERATION: plan your outgoings so that they are sufficient

for you and others and do not be wasteful.
DILIGENCE: do not waste time and always do something useful.
Do not do anything which is not necessary.
SINCERITY: do not be led astray by being evasive.
Innocence and truth must rule your thoughts and your speech.

As you might imagine, the aesthetic code of nihilist men and women was extremely functional and modest and outlined with great precision what clothes were to be worn, what colour they should be, what sort of apartment you should have and so on. A parting down the back of the head for men or backcombed hair in women was considered vulgar. No one was supposed to wear gold chains, bracelets, colourful dresses with jewellery or top hats; any sign of luxury in your apartment was considered reprehensible. In this respect, the nihilists anticipated the standard attire in the Komsomol of the twentieth century. The only difference was that the Soviet youngsters were incredibly resentful of this enforced uniform, whereas the young radicals of the 1860s wore their grey coats with pride.

The trend for dark clothing, among both men and women, was initially determined by three factors: practicality, modesty (in contrast to the affectations of the hated nobility) and the influence of a seminary education on many members of the movement. One of the most original characterics of the nihilists' fashion sense was their demonstrative disregard for warm clothing. In the winter it was acceptable to make a summer coat warmer by throwing a blanket over it, which was believed to be healthier and more hygienic. The story is told that once, during a cold snap, Chernyshevsky, who hadn't been informed of the new Realist dress code, offered some money to a young man wrapped in a blanket so that he could buy himself something warmer to wear. Describing the topics of discussion during the Realists' meetings, one of the participants, a certain Skabichevksy, wrote that:

"Much of our teatime was devoted to discussions about what types of food should be considered essential, and what types a luxury. Caviar and sardines were met with a unanimous ban. There was no agreement on the subject of herrings and apples, as the herring makes up a worker's regular lunch menu, while not even a pauper would say 'no' to an apple. Wines were definitively prohibited, while vodka and beer were allowed – again because they offered the only joy in this life for millions of ordinary, working class people. Tobacco was subjected to a double sanction: despite the fact that people of all social classes smoke, even a puritan like Rakhmetov (the mysterious superman from *What Is To Be Done?*) would allow himself to smoke a cigar on occasion, and an expensive one at that."

The nihilists' attitude to art and culture was just as severe. Bazarov himself says: "A good chemist is twenty times as useful as any poet," although he himself is a literary creation. Another, equally shocking 'anti-cultural' phrase was attributed to Pisarev, the chief ideologist of

Alexander II Tsar of Russia (1818–1881).
Vanity Fair – No 50
Sovereigns No 4 – La civilisation russe, 1869.
Original Artwork:
Cartoon by Coide.
Photo by Hulton Archive / Getty Images

THE REFORMS OF ALEXANDER II (1855–1870)

When Nicholas I died in 1855, not only was the Russian economy in trouble but the country was utterly isolated after the Crimean War – no wonder Nicholas I is so often compared to Vladimir Putin. His son Alexander II initiated a long overdue programme of reforms as soon as he was crowned. The most important of these was undoubtedly the abolition of serfdom, which won him the nickname the Tsar-Liberator, but other modernisations, like a new penal code and (limited) self-government, were vital in transforming Russia from a feudal state into something like a modern, capitalist one.

the 'thinking Realists': "A pair of boots is of more use than all the works of Shakespeare." Pisarev was no boor, it is just that he thought of the interaction between ethics and aesthetics in a specific way: "The end result of all the thoughts and actions of every honest man should be to solve once and for all the inescapable problem of our hungry and poorly clothed people; there is nothing beyond this problem which is worthy of our worries, thoughts and actions."

Accordingly, 'good' art was supposed to be put to immediate use in changing the reality of the poor. Poetry and Shakespeare could without a doubt be part of this process.

The nihilists were not only irritated by anything that was deemed to be useless and elitist, but especially by the aristocratic character of 'high' art. As Kropotkin said, "The nihilists hated the endless talk of beauty, ideals, aesthetics and art for art's sake, while every piece of art could be bought for money which had been squeezed from the starving peasants and the downtrodden workers."

One of the most scandalous and most discussed aspects of Russian nihilism was its attitude to people's private lives. After *What Is To Be Done?* became a guiding light for the freedom loving youth, they started embracing the emancipation of women and free love, casting off the chains of matrimony and living communally in dormitories instead of in strict family units. A certain 27-year-old writer, Vasily Sleptsov, was one of those who decided to put Chernyshevsky's theories of communality into practice. He rented a large apartment on Znamenskaya Street in St Petersburg and invited his like-minded male and female friends to live there. The city was immediately alive with obscene rumours about orgies. The women gradually left the commune and a year later it foundered completely.

This radical experiment in women's equality failed but relations among the sexes began to change, even if in a less scandalous context. Ideas of female emancipation became incredibly popular. This process followed two different paths – in society and in the family – but in both cases women fought for the right to make their own decisions. The path to autonomy seemed clear: education and, if she's lucky, a job, a career and an independent standing in society. When it came to personal happiness, things took a more exotic turn with the female nihilists. Inspired by the love plot of *What Is To Be Done?*, fictitious marriages became very popular. They freed women from domestic slavery and permitted them to maintain their standing in a patriarchal society. In any case, as was observed by their contemporaries, only very few young women went along with such risky arrangements. These young Realists of the 1860s were true pioneers of Russian feminism.

Last but not least, we come to the political activity of the nihilists, and there's an important caveat here; the nihilists tolerated the name which the writer Turgenev had tagged them with in everyday life, but when it came to politics they were categorically against it, preferring the more appropriate 'revolutionaries' or 'revolutionary democrats'. We should also remember that the revolutionary struggle of the radicals of the 1860s was playing out in the midst of the largest and undoubtedly most progressive reforms of Alexander II – most notably the abolition of serfdom in 1861. These reforms undermined the nihilists' agenda for change somewhat, but they also spurred them on. The original nihilist political organisation was called 'Land and Freedom'. Inspired by the ideas of Herzen and Chernyshevsky, it existed from 1861 to 1864, fuelled by the futile hope that the peasants, now freed by the tsar's decree, would seize the land for themselves and start a popular uprising against autocracy and private ownership. The nihilists waited in vain: the peasants were grateful and obedient to the tsar and behaved accordingly.

Instead of slipping into obscurity, however, the nihilists showed society that they were not only promiscuous but criminal too. It was in response to the series of assassinations and bombings which the nihilists unleashed that some of the greatest Russian novels were written, as their

Self-portrait in watercolour. Mikhail Bakunin, 1839

MIKHAIL BAKUNIN (1814–1876) AND ALEXANDER HERZEN (1812–1870)

The careers of these two brilliant revolutionary aristocrats unfolded in parallel: starting out together in the same pro-European circles, they came under the influence of French utopian socialists, English economists and German philosophers, before emigrating to Europe during Nicholas I repressions of the 1840s, where they witnessed the 1848 revolution and its violent suppression. Later their paths diverged: Herzen went to London, where he became an influential author and publisher, while Bakunin remained on the continent with the local radicals, laying the foundations of of both anarchism and panslavism.

Girl-student. Nikolai Yaroshenko, 1883.
Courtesy of the Kaluga Museum of Fine Arts, Kaluga, Russia

authors spoke out against the subculture. The most famous of these is Dostoevsky's *The Possessed* (1871). The main character, the villainous Peter Verkhovensky, was inspired by real-life revolutionary Sergei Nechaev. Another character, Ivan Shatov, was based on Ivan Ivanov, the student who was murdered by Nechaev for speaking out against Nechaev's radical propaganda – the incident which had provided the initial impetus for Dostoevsky's novel. Dostoevsky uses Shatov, a disillusioned rebel, to voice many of his own ideals.

Following the murder, Nechaev fled abroad where he turned to the patriarchs of Russian political exile, Mikhail Bakunin and Alexander Herzen, for help. They were unimpressed, deeming him to be dishonest and fanatical. During an investigation into his activities, Nechaev wrote *The Catechism of a Revolutionary* in which, among other things, he proclaimed: "The revolutionary is a doomed man. He has no private interests, no affairs, sentiments, ties, property nor even a name of his own. His entire being is devoured by one purpose, one thought, one passion – the Revolution. Heart and soul, not merely in word but in deed, he has severed every link with the social order and with the entire civilised world; with the laws, good manners, conventions, and morality of that world. He is its merciless enemy and continues to inhabit it with only one purpose – to destroy it."

Public opinion responded to Nechaev's hostility in kind: Switzerland handed him over to Russia to mete out its own justice and he was imprisoned in the Peter and Paul Fortress as a common criminal and died there in 1882.

At the end of the 1860s and start of the 1870s the revolutionary *raznochintsy* and their spawn, the nihilists, dwindled away. Following an assassination attempt on the tsar and Nechaev's imprisonment, radical cells around the country were crushed and, more importantly, the movement itself lost face in the eyes of a previously sympathetic public. There were no more revivals of classical 'Bazarovian' nihilism among Russian youth. However, nihilism's evergreen postulate – that 'nothing is sacred' – continues to dominate life in Russia to this day.

Arrest of a Propagandist. Ilya Repin, 1880-89. Courtesy of the State Tretyakov Gallery, Moscow

CHAPTER 3

Free Radicals: Populists, Marxists and Reactionaries. 1870–1905

The 1870s was an incredibly turbulent and self-contradictory decade, culminating in the assassination of Tsar Alexander III in 1881. This period also saw a blossoming in mainstream 'classical' Russian culture, including the publication of Tolstoy's *Anna Karenina* (1877) and Dostoevsky's *The Brothers Karamazov* (1880) and the debut of operas by Mussorgsky and Rimsky-Korsakov. The emancipation of the serfs was followed by progressive reforms in education, self-government and the military. A basic understanding of civic rights was emerging in Russia, along with the institutions to support it.

However, despite the gradual expansion of these freedoms, the 1870s saw the birth of new protest movements, both violent and nonviolent, and the continuation of the rebellions – from Poland to Lake Baikal – strikes and peasant unrest that had characterised the 1860s. No less than six assassinations attempts were made on the tsar, alongside more successful attacks on governors-general and police chiefs. All this in the reign of the so-called Tsar Liberator! Ironically, there had been very little unrest under the reign of his father, the paranoid and conservative Nicholas I, who never did anything good for his country. One can draw some very unhappy conclusions here: not about the personalities of members of the Romanov family, but about Russia itself. What sort of country is it where, with the appearance of a ruler who is kind and liberal and wants his people to have more freedom, those very people rise up as one to demand his extermination, whereas under the rule of dictators, villains and bullies, the same people obediently keep their heads down? Are the apologists for Stalin – or his present-day caricature, Putin – really right when they say that harsh rule is the only thing Russians understand? That, as the poet Nikolai Nekrasov said, "The harsher the punishment, the quieter the people"? Is freedom really worth less than cheap vodka? Alas, it seems that history proves this to be the case, although in my mind and heart I can't help but resist this idea.

For the youth of Russia, however, Alexander's reforms offered many new opportunities: the *raznochintsy* and minor nobility tried out new, rather attractive, walks of life. No longer limited to being army officers, clerks or civil servants, they could become engineers, lawyers, agriculturalists and even entrepreneurs. Many took full advantage of this, actively participating in the construction of a new, capitalist Russia.

History doesn't tell us whether they had their own organisations, social circles or clubs; most probably they didn't. Organically integrated into the 'positive' governmental doctrine, they didn't need another identity. The most famous literary heroes of the period – like Raskolnikov from *Crime and Punishment* or Prince Myshkin from *The Idiot* – did not inspire copycats like Bazarov had (although an 'idiot' subculture might have been fun).

The passionate, progressive minority did not disappear, but by the turn of the 1870s it was demoralised: Chernyshevsky was in prison, Dobrolyubov and Pisarev had died young and the Nechaev incident had ruined the radicals' reputation. As is so often the case, the pendulum of thought swung sharply in the opposite direction – away from nihilistic rejection and towards an all-encompassing love for 'the people', known in Russian as the *narod*. This was in many ways a logical step: until then all reformist and revolutionary movements in Russia, starting with the Decembrists, had acted for the people but not with the people. But the young people of the 1870s saw isolation from their deeper roots and estrangement from popular wisdom as the reason for their predecessors' failure. The members of this new movement came to be known as Populists (*narodniki*) – a sort of brand name which united many different circles and movements.

The groups making up the Populists movement differed in how radical they were. There were those of a more conservative bent, including many former Slavophiles. The priority for them was to get in touch with their roots at any cost and learn true morality from the people. Then there were the more pragmatic reformist-liberals, who also wanted to soak up the people's wisdom, but as part of a move towards gradual socio-economic reform. Slightly more radical still was the 'propagandist' arm of the Populists, personified by the bearded philosopher and sociologist Pyotr Lavrov. He was in favour of revolution, but thought that people weren't ready for it, so progressive intellectuals should actively try to enlighten them with propaganda. The most extreme Populists were known as the 'conspiratorialists' or 'anarchists'. Their first leader was a former comrade of Nechaev, Pyotr Tkachev; he did not really believe in the revolutionary potential of the common people, or in the stability of an autocratic regime, so he tried to create an underground organisation that could seize power and create a communist-style state. He was arrested in the early 1870s; after spending a year and a half in prison, he emigrated and died in Paris aged 42.

The strongest branch of Populism was the Anarchists. The history of anarchism in Russia is fairly paradoxical: the world's two greatest theorists of anarchism were Russian – Mikhail Bakunin and Pyotr Kropotkin – but they were aristocrats who spent very little time in Russia and had negligible influence on revolutionary practice there, at least in the nineteenth century. Kropotkin was, however, involved in the conception of the most significant campaign in the history of Populism. As part of a group called the 'Great society of Propaganda', which sought to bring together different Populist groups in order to awaken the people's rebellious instincts, he helped to organise what was known as the 'Going to the People' in the spring and summer of 1874. Around three thousand young intellectuals, students and even school children, dressed in simple peasant clothes, went out into the villages of European Russia to spread the word. They talked to the villagers, persuading them of the need to rise up in rebellion in order to achieve a better life. The propagandists pointed out the obvious shortcomings of the land reforms and the importance of dividing the land more equitably. But the people themselves turned out to be a bitter disappointment. They were sceptical about revolutionary thought and unreceptive to calls to rebel. Worse still, some locals informed the authorities about the activists and the campaign ended with mass arrests and the confiscation of campaign literature.

Vasily Andreyev – populariser of the balalaika, 1880s

The distinctive look of the Populist activists is captured in Ilya Repin's famous painting *Arrest of a Propagandist* (1892): the propagandist, held by the watchful gendarmes, is not dressed like any city-dweller of the times – be that a student, 'new man' or aristocrat. He is wearing a bright red shirt with baggy trousers tucked into his boots. In part, this style of dress, typical for villages and working suburbs, acted as a disguise – an attempt by the Populist agitators to be taken for a member of the people; but it also reflects a fashion for anything rustic, 'native' and homespun, just like the kaftans and *murmolka* of the Slavophile Aksakov. This subcultural code extended to language – the Populists slogan was "Down with French, long live simple Russian!" – and also to painting and music.

Repin was a member of a group of painters known as the 'Wanderers', who effectively represented a Populist faction in the world of fine art. Besides the subject matter of the paintings, which often depicted scenes from the lives of peasants and labourers in a realistic fashion, their version of 'going to the people' manifested itself in the organisation of travelling exhibitions in provincial cities and even villages. Before the Wanderers, there had emerged in music a group of talented composers, dubbed 'The Mighty Handful', whose populism manifested itself, first and foremost, in the subject matter of their operas, which drew on Russian epics and fairy tales. The influence of folk music on their work is more questionable, although there are some fantastic examples of that too, such as the 'Polovtsian dances' from Alexander Borodin's opera *Prince Igor*.

The Populist tendency in music also gave rise to a less well-known phenomenon – faux-folk songs. The shocking truth is that the three most widely known Russian folk songs – *Kalinka*, *The Pedlars* (*Korobeiniki*) and *The Cudgel* (*Dubinushka)* were actually composed by professional musicians in the 1870s and 1880s. Worse still, the balalaika – the legendary Russian folk instrument with a triangular body and three strings – was, it appears, created or recreated, by the musicians Vasily Andreyev and Franz Paserbsky. The empathetic intelligentsia was putting its own finishing touches on folk masterpieces.

The favourite faux-folk song of the militant Populist youth was *The Cudgel* and its refrain "Hey, *dubi-i-nushka*, hey ho!" became something like a revolutionary call to arms. The story goes that when a Populist rebel by the name of Fyodor Yurkovsky – then famous under the nom de guerre 'Sashka the Engineer' – was executing a spy named Tavleev in the garden of an Odessa restaurant, a group of youths sang *The Cudgel* to drown out the bloodbath. Yurkovsky, now largely forgotten, was a legendary figure at the time: one of only a few Populists to turn to terrorism, he organised Russia's first 'revolutionary expropriation' – that is, robbing a bank to pay the revolution's expenses. He was also the first to wear the revolutionary's uniform of a stiff dark suit with a dagger tucked into the waist and a revolver in the waistcoat pocket. Yurkovsky's violent tactics were rare, however: the Populists' preference was to incite eventual revolution by bringing enlightenment to the masses. "You terrorists are worse than the monarchists!" Yurkovsky was once told by a fellow Populist Andrei Zhelyabov, who nevertheless went on to kill Alexander II. Times were changing.

The epilogue of the 'Going to the People' campaign and other similar attempts at enlightenment of the people was the sadly notorious 'Trial of the 193' in 1877 and 1878. The wave of arrests – and remember that this was under a more liberal tsar – lasted several years. Around 900 Populists activists were detained along with 8,000 sympathisers. Most of them were released without charge, but 770 were held under investigation and 47 died during or immediately after the investigation. Twelve committed suicide and 38 went mad. Of the Populists arrested, 193 were taken to trial, most of them in their twenties. Only three of them pleaded guilty. Not one of the prisoners, including fifteen women, asked for clemency. In 1878 events took a dramatic and rapid turn in a very different direction. The 'gentle' phase of Populism – the fervent proselytising and courting of the peasants – seemed ridiculous after the Trial of the 193. In 1876 an underground youth organisation called 'Land and Liberty' had been created (a different organisation from the one established in the 1860s). It was founded on principles of strict secrecy, clear hierarchy, and majority rule. It was governed by its 'Administration', by specially targeted groups among the workers in the countryside and by the so-called 'disorganisers' – a sort of rapid response unit which would hurry to join any incident of popular unrest, then aggravate the problems and obstruct government forces.

Vera Zasulich, 1900s

Land and Liberty was dedicated to the task of popular revolution. Their preferred method was known as 'settled propaganda': agitators did not 'go to the people' but actually lived among them in villages, stirring up the workers and carrying out acts of retribution against the authorities.

It was Land and Liberty which held the first ever political demonstration in Russian history, on 6 December 1876 in front of the Kazan Cathedral in St Petersburg. One of those who spoke to the crowd was 19-year-old Marxist Georgy Plekhanov, Lenin's future mentor. However, the repercussions of this historical event were minute when compared to the organisation's next high-profile act – an assassination attempt on the mayor of St Petersburg, Fyodor Trepov. In February 1878, Vera Zasulich, the 28-year-old daughter of an impoverished Polish noble, booked an appointment with Trepov. There she shot him in the stomach three times, gravely wounding but not killing him. Zasulich was arrested and put on trial. Russia, and indeed the whole world, was astounded when the court then acquitted her. This might be the first time that the haughty West looked at Russia and saw a modern, civilised country. The court found that the assassination attempt was an 'act of retaliation' against the cruel governor who, the year before, had illegally given the order to flog a Populist who refused to take his hat off. Corporal punishment had been prohibited by Alexander II. The emperor was extremely displeased at the acquittal and the justice minister was forced to resign, but Zasulich managed to escape to Switzerland before the case was reopened.

Assassination attempts – some successful, some not – continued throughout 1878. The governor-general of Kharkov and several high ranking police officials in Kiev and St Petersburg died at the hands of Land and Liberty's marksmen and bombers. At the same time the society continued their propaganda work, publishing magazines and newspapers, sowing the seeds of revolutionary thought among the workers and the peasants. This was undoubtedly a contradictory methodology. In the summer of 1879, an underground meeting of Land and Liberty held in Voronezh sparked a split in the organisation: the moderate wing, including Plekhanov and, oddly, Zasulich, opposed the direct action that others favoured. A month later and Land and Liberty was no more, with members of the moderate wing forming a new organisation called the 'Black Repartition' which concentrated on educating the peasants by publishing a new newspaper called *The Kernel* (*Zerno*).

Their more radical opponents formed a sort of union of terrorists, an organisation that was destined to be both infamous and tragic and which they called the 'People's Will'. A century after these events, the Soviet writer Yuri Trifonov wrote a novel about the People's Will and called it *The Impatient Ones*. The word 'impatient' seems appropriate: they were driven not so much by their intolerance of the oppression of the poor classes, as by a sense of urgency. "While grass grows," as Hamlet said "The steed starves". Like the Decembrists, the activists of the People's Will loved the common people and had infinite sympathy

SOFIA PEROVSKAYA (1853–1881) and ANDREI ZHELYABOV (1851–1881)

A truly heroic pair of terrorist and regicides – a Russian Bonnie and Clyde, but with a political agenda. She was from an old noble family and the daughter of a one-time governor of St Petersburg; he was from a family of peasant serfs. They met in prison in their early twenties and in 1881 they masterminded the assassination of Alexander II, although it was Perovskaya who gave the order for the attack after Zhelyabov was arrested two days previously. They were hanged side by side.

The Conspiracies at St Petersburg: the Nihilists on the Scaffold.
The Illustrated London News, 30 April 1881

with them – but they didn't really believe in them. Their attitude was: why wait for the workers and peasants to be sufficiently tutored in political consciousness to rise up? They preferred to act themselves, although they were in a small minority and their methods were very controversial. Impatience is a popular and infectious emotion, so while Land and Liberty only had two hundred odd members, the People's Will managed to create around eighty local cells, served by five hundred activists and thousands of sympathisers. Their main aim was to kill the tsar: from the autumn of 1879 onwards, the People's Will carried out five assassination attempts. This all happened against a background of peasant uprisings, factory strikes and rising discontent in the country. As Minister of Interior Pyotr Valuyev wrote in his diary, "A sort of undefined discontent has gripped everyone and is evident in every class of society. Everyone has something to complain about; it is as if they desire change and are waiting for it." Meanwhile, the tsar, according to Valuyev "…seems tired and talks of the state of his nerves … the monarchy is half-collapsed." The People's Will finally succeeded in killing Alexander II on 1 March 1881.

The assassination was masterminded by Sofia Perovskaya – one of the most enchanting women in Russia's rich history. The daughter of a former governor of St Petersburg, she was just 27 when she was hanged in April 1881, but was already a veteran of the Going to the People, the Trial of the 193 and every previous attempt on the life of the tsar. On 1 March it was she who waved a white handkerchief to give the signal for bomb-throwers to attack the tsar's carriage on the streets of St Petersburg. After the explosion, she stood at first rooted to the spot in a state of shock, but soon fled. She could have escaped the capital if she had not stayed in the city hoping to save her arrested comrades, including her common-law husband, the former serf and one-time opponent of terrorism Andrei Zhelyabov (29). Zhelyabov had been detained two days before the assassination, but he still volunteered to be executed, alongside Perovskaya and the other assassins: Nikolai Kibalchich (27), a brilliant engineer who drew a plan for a jet-powered space rocket while in prison, Nikolai Rysakov (20), and Timofei Mikhailov (22). The suicide bomber Ignaty Grinevitsky (24), who died along with Alexander II, wrote in his will shortly before the assassination: "Fate has doomed me to an early death. I will not see us succeed, I will not live one day or one hour in that happy time of celebration, but I believe that by my death I will have done everything that I had to do."

The execution took place on the morning of 3 April 1881. The five convicted members were driven through St Petersburg in open carts. A sixth, Gesia Gelfman, 26, who was pregnant, had her execution postponed. The crowd that turned up to watch them was divided: one poor woman who waved a white flag at the carts was attacked, but others, according to future revolutionary Andrei Breitfus, then a teenager, were surprised to see that the regicides had such young, handsome faces and were not enraged, but puzzled and saddened by their actions. Renowned actress Maria Savina, who was following the procession from the balcony of her apartment, claimed that, apart from one of those convicted, Rysakov, the faces of the others who were being dragged to their execution were "fairer and merrier than those which surrounded them."

I will venture to express a politically incorrect theory here: terrorism is not an absolute evil, but a phenomenon with its own historical and moral nuances. Can one think of the People's Will as equivalent to the Norwegian terrorist and mass murderer of children, Anders Breivik? Or Islamist fanatics who blow hundreds of innocent people to bits? I don't agree with the actions of the People's Will, especially since they brought no positive results, but I cannot deny that these people had noble motives, rational minds and that they exhibited a certain personal heroism. And I understand them on an emotional level too: their actions came from their intolerance of a desperate situation. It's easy to accuse them of bloodshed, of inefficiency, and of an inaccurate assessment of the situation – but there is another logic at play here, best expressed in the revolutionary mantra "Soyons réalistes, exigeons l'impossible!" – let's be realists and demand the impossible.

Sofia Perovskaya wrote: "We have begun a great thing. Perhaps it will take more than one generation to carry it through, but it must be done." These words could serve as the epigraph to everything that was epic and romantic in the nineteenth century, when young people were altruistic, un-encumbered by material values and armed with a strong sense of their own mission. They may have been a minority, but they did exist. Russia has never been a democratic country and its history has always been created by a small minority. Most often, this minority has been hideous, but some-times, just sometimes, they have been exquisite.

Marxists and Reactionaries

The long-awaited murder of the tsar turned out to be a double blow for the People's Will: it lost its charismatic leaders and it discovered that the public sympathised with the murdered reformer-tsar, who had even stopped to help a guard injured in the initial attack. The assassination was a strategic blunder by the People's Will. Nevertheless, immediately after the attack, the surviving members of the executive Committee of the People's Will issued an ultimatum to the new tsar and his government, saying: "If the government doesn't change its politics, revolution will be inevitable. The government must express the will of the people." Their confidence was misplaced: what followed was a period of arrests and trials, of exiles and emigrations, and of waning enthusiasm. What is more, the new tsar, Alexander III, by nature a conservative, was convinced that liberalism had been his father's downfall and so pursued a tough policy, strengthening both autocracy and Russian orthodoxy. Although unpopular, unlike his grandfather Nicholas I, who had led Russia into total stagnation and degradation, Alexander III was a very effective leader and implemented social, economic and financial reforms which significantly improved the lives and working conditions of the peasants and particularly workers in towns. The amelioration in conditions, along with a rigorous clamp-down on protests, meant that unrest in the early 1880s quickly died out.

The swan song of revolutionary terrorism was the planned assassination of Alexander III, set to take place on 1 March 1887, organised by a group of students who gave themselves the rather grand title 'the Terrorist Faction of the People's Will'. Among their members was a 21-year-old named Alexander Ulyanov, the older brother of Vladimir Ulyanov, better known as Lenin. The tsar was merciless in punishing this failed attempt, despite the fact that it went no further than buying explosives with money raised from the sale of gold medals that Alexander Ulyanov had won at school. All the conspirators were hanged. But, as Russians like to joke, the younger brother got his revenge in the end.

As the urban working class grew in size Marxism became increasingly popular among Russian revolutionaries. In the 1880s and 1890s a controversy arose among radical intellectuals, much as it had back in the 1840s between the *zapadniki* and the Slavophiles. The Populists continued to stand up for the peasants and believed that socialism would come to Russia after a rural uprising. One of their most persuasive arguments was the fact that about 90% of the population lived in rural areas – these were the 'people' that needed to be helped. They could not deny the growth of the proletariat in the cities but they believed that this, like capitalism, was happening artificially. The Marxists, by contrast, laid their bets on the urban working class because they were more progressive, had no property and were capable of organising themselves. The first Marxist

GEORGY PLEKHANOV (1856–1918)

The first true Russian Marxist philosopher and co-founder of the Bolshevik party (although he didn't stay there long), Plekhanov began as a Populist in Land and Liberty, but always rejected terrorism in favour of politics and propaganda. At 24, fearing arrest and a life of hard labour, he emigrated using false documents and then spent most of the rest of his life abroad. He had a complicated relationship with Lenin: he was his chief mentor in philosophy and political economy, but did not approve of his tactics and condemned the October Revolution as premature and dangerous.

Supporters of Nestor Makhno, 1919

Makhno in a fur cap, 1919

group, 'Emancipation of Labour', was created by Plekhanov in Geneva in 1883. In Russia itself it was not until 1895 that a number of Marxist groupings, which included among their number 25-year-old Vladimir Ulyanov, created the 'League for the emancipation of the working Class', which became the Russian Social Democratic Labour Party (RSDLP) and, ultimately, the Communist Party.

It was at the RSDLP's Second Congress in London in 1903 that the party became split between a minority, who believed any revolution would have to be preceded by a stage of capitalism, and the majority who believed in immediate proletarian revolution. The former became known as the 'Mensheviks' (from the Russian word for minority) and argued for parliamentary politics and progressive coalitions; the latter took their name from the Russian word for majority – they were the 'Bolsheviks'. The rest, as they say, is history.

In the early 1900s, however, the Bolsheviks were far from the only game in town. Out of the ashes of the People's Will had risen the 'Socialist Revolutionary Party' (known as the SRs), which continued its policies of peasant socialism and intermittent terrorism and pursued a fierce rivalry with the Social Democrats. A third, more romantic, party were the anarchists, inspired by the émigré Kropotkin. While the Social Democrats and SRs dominated in the cold, working class capitals of Moscow and St Petersburg, the anarchists flourished in the temperamental southern regions of Ukraine and Georgia, as well as in Belarus and Bessarabia, with their large populations of young Jewish would-be revolutionaries. The anarchists enjoyed a boost in support across the country when revolution eventually did come to Russia, albeit in attenuated form, in 1905. By 1907 there were anarchist organisations in 225 settlements throughout Russia, home to 7,000 anarchists whose average age was under 20, according to witnesses. Thanks to their inherent resistance to authority, the term anarchist encompassed an enormous variety of movements, ranging from the 'mystic anarchists', who included St Petersburg poets like Vyacheslav Ivanov, to violent anarchy-communist revolutionaries such as the 'Black Banner' terrorist group or the infamous and charismatic Nestor Makhno, who was arrested for the first time in 1906, aged 18. These newly emergent left-wing organisations found themselves in conflict not only with the police, the army and the Cossacks, but also another voluntary force of pro-tsarist reaction and racism – the 'Black Hundreds'. This was a rare example – perhaps unique in the history of Russia – in which a nationwide grassroots group appeared which was not so much a youth movement as an anti-youth movement. I am reminded of the old Monty Python sketch in which 'Hell's Grannies' beat up punks and bikers with their umbrellas and knitting needles. The Black Hundreds were not grannies but artisans, janitors, traders, policemen, low-ranking clergy, thieves – a motley collection of the scum of the city, united in their pride at being Russian and Orthodox. They targeted revolutionaries, liberals, intellectuals, Jews and students.

They beat, robbed and killed them. Jews tended to live in communities, so finding and attacking them and at the same time plundering their shops and apartments was easy – it was called a *pogrom*. Activists were attacked at meetings and rallies. Students, who had to wear a uniform and thus were easily identified, were simply jumped on in the street. The Black Hundreds, who took their name from a seventeenth-century patriotic organisation, were ultra-conservative and ultra-primitive. Mikhail Druzhinin, one of their leaders, said: "It is a sacred Russian duty to exterminate revolutionaries! You know who they are and where to find them. Death to revolutionaries and the Jews." The Black Hundreds' slogan put it in even simpler terms: "Kill the Jews and save Russia!" On the whole the Russian elite, and especially the nobility and the clergy, sympathised with them, and they enjoyed the patronage of Grand Duke Sergei, the uncle of Tsar Nicholas II, who had acceded to the throne in 1894. While Nicholas's government could not openly condone their violence and lawlessness, the Ministry of the Interior secretly funded right-wing fundamentalists and helped them out if they got into trouble. It is to the credit of Russia's young that they had hardly anything to do with the Black Hundreds. Neither did the peasantry, who had little occasion to meet either revolutionaries or Jews, who were forbidden from working the land. As for educated Russians, it would simply have been very uncool to sympathise with the thuggish, semiliterate Black Hundreds: all of the humanitarian leading lights of the day, including Tolstoy, Gorky and Chekhov, were violently opposed to them. The Black Hundreds reached the peak of their popularity during the sluggish revolution of 1905, after which the movement slowly died out, scandal-ridden and despised. Recently, however, they have enjoyed a revival, with the blessing of Vladimir Putin.

Of course, the members of all the political circles and groups mentioned above only constituted a tiny, if vociferous, proportion of the young people of Russia at the turn of the century. So what were the rest doing and thinking? The answer is: not very much. The reign of Alexander III had seen an economic boom, with particular growth in industry, banking and construction, and young people's ambitions were mostly oriented towards their careers. The idealism of the Realists and Populists gave way to the pragmatism of the first Russian yuppies – engineers, lawyers and clerks. The more conscientious were adherents of the so-called 'theory of small deeds', first formulated in the early 1880s. As the one 'big deed', the revolution preached by Perovskaya, had proved to be unfeasible, liberals suggested exchanging it for a multitude of small deeds. Progressive writers of the time enjoined educated citizens not to forget the hardships of the peasants and workers, and to help them as much as they could: to teach, to heal and to explain to them how to adapt to the complexities of modern life. It was a bit like the Going to the People but without the political agenda; it enjoyed the support of Tolstoy, who was also calling for a new union with the people. The theory of small deeds has continued to flourish in Russia, whenever the country is going through periods of reaction and cannot really do anything about it.

Throughout the nineteenth century, political subcultures were closely linked with developments in art and literature, spawning manifestos, philosophies and conspiracies. But between the demise of Populism and the twin shocks of the First World War and the 1917 Revolution, this close association slowly disintegrated. Youth movements became purely political or boringly bureaucratic and they lost their subcultural feel; meanwhile, artists, writers and musicians also went their own way, preaching new ideas about 'pure art' and calling for a break from the uninspiring reality around them. It's interesting to note that this division of labour brought impressive results. In 1917 Russian revolutionaries became the first in history to be utterly victorious in their aims, while the artists – what came to be known as the Russian avant-garde – also became famous the world over.

Portrait of Natalia Goncharova, Mikhail Larionov, 1915. Courtesy of the State Tretyakov Gallery, Moscow

CHAPTER 4

Brave New World: Cults, Mysticism and the Art of the Silver Age. 1905–1930

In the nineteenth century the men and women of Russia's subcultures – be they artists or terrorists – had been fired with romanticism, but they had remained realists nonetheless: even the hopeless revolt of the Decembrists and the suicidal actions of the People's Will had been founded on concrete expectations and calculations – often inaccurate ones – about the common good. Socialism and Marxism had grown from the philosophical foundation laid by the enlightenment, and the slow but steady development of a capitalist sensibility had produced new economic conditions and a new way of life. But what had the passionate and peculiar rebels really achieved? Not much. Accordingly, in the early twentieth century, many young people became disenchanted with the materialist agenda. Large numbers of thoughtful Russians lost faith in the idea of making a new, more equitable Russia, and so decided to wage a battle for spiritual renewal instead. In doing so, they drew on a centuries-old tradition of popular religious dissent in Russia.

Cults and Mysticism

The story of sects and cults in Russia is an old one. In the middle of the seventeenth century there was a schism in the Russian Orthodox Church between the official church and the so-called 'Old Believers', who rejected innovations in the liturgy. Sometime later, other, smaller breakaway sects emerged in the countryside, like the self-flagellating 'Khlysty' and the self-mutilating 'Skoptsy'; they were followed by pacifist groups like the 'Dukhobory' and the 'Molokane' and 'Western' non-conformists like the 'Baptists' and 'Adventists'.

By 1917, there were around one million members of so-called sects, which is to say, Christian confessions outside the Russian Orthodox Church, and they were by no means confined to distant villages. Philosopher Nikolai Berdyaev blamed the popularity of alternative religion on failings within the established church itself: "The cult member is a stricken man, a man who is wounded by the untruths of the Orthodox way of life and of the dogma of the Church." It is true that the reputation of priests had for a long time been very bad: they were seen as sinners, drunkards, gluttons and bribe-takers. Many devout believers were struck by the contrast between the priestly ideal and reality, and resented it. But the people needed God and so they found alternatives. Berdyaev divided sects into two basic categories: those who searched for the truth and thirsted to do good works, like the 'Dukhobory and the Tolstoyans', who followed the teachings of the great novelist, and those who were looking for religious passion and ecstasy, like the Khlysty. The former worshipped by preaching and prayer, the latter by sacred and often erotic rites with pagan roots. Berdyaev described them as 'orgiastic'. The state-run Orthodox Church waged a continuous war on the sects, seeking to turn their adherents into social outcasts. The sects responded with unruliness. It is not surprising, therefore, that, in response to the revolutionary events of the beginning of the century, one of Tsar Nicholas II's first liberal reforms was the 'Edict of Tolerance of April 1905', which gave legal rights to Old Believers and other religious dissidents. Following this decree, sectarianism flourished. If Christian sects were, to quote Marx, "the opium of the people", then at the turn of the century the opium of the intelligentsia, along with Marxism, anarchism and so on, was mysticism. Spiritual circles and lodges devoted to esoteric knowledge became as important a part of the leisure time of the urban elite of the early twentieth century as literary salons had been at the start of the nineteenth. The intelligentsia and some of the nobility, disillusioned with church dogmas, actively took part in what was known as 'God-seeking' – and in the most exotic places.

Portrait of Grigory Rasputin,
1910s

While the spiritual dissidents of the nineteenth century had turned to Catholicism, the new generation discovered paganism and, more importantly, eastern religions like Buddhism and Hinduism, which until then had been virtually unknown in Russia. Gurus and holy Mahatmas began to prosper in the icy north. The cult figures (in every sense) who intrigued Russians with their mystic teachings at this time included the Theosophist Helena Blavatsky, who authored works such as *The Secret Doctrine* and *The Voice of Silence* and captivated Tolstoy and Kandinsky among others, and George Gurdjieff, an occult adventurer, dancer and author of the theory of the 'fourth way'. Further evidence of the vogue for spiritualism and esotericism can be seen in the phenomenal importance of another figure – Grigory Rasputin. This 'man of God', presumed to have been a member of the Khlysty, was a favourite of the tsar's family and exerted great influence not only on spiritual affairs in the country but on the socio-political situation too.

It appears that Russian society at the start of the twentieth century really was sick. But 'sick' does not necessarily mean boring or talentless: the paradoxical experience of Russia has proved many times that when the country is in a pitiful state it is not only revolutionaries who are inspired, but artists too.

The Silver Age

The Russian cultural revolution of the late nineteenth and early twentieth centuries was wholly bloodless and not driven by any anxiety for the common good. The word 'freedom' did play an important part in the motivations of the participants in this revolution, but this did not mean political or economic freedom inasmuch as creative freedom, spiritual impulsiveness and, above all else, individual liberty. The instruments used to acquire this sought-after freedom – the entry ticket to an ideal new world – were not guns, protests and strikes but the pen, the brush and the image. This era has come to be known as the 'Silver Age', a response to the 'Golden Age' of Russian literature in the early nineteenth century, the era of Pushkin and his contemporaries. The Silver Age stretches from about 1895 to… well, actually, it's quite hard to pinpoint an exact time, but I would stretch this glorious era up to 1930. In contrast to its golden predecessor, the Silver Age was not purely literary but was also marked by achievements of global significance in painting, theatre, choreography, architecture, music, cinema and photography. The creative people who made the Silver Age did not belong to any official organisations – at least not before the 1920s – but instead tended to form small literary and artistic circles in Moscow and especially St Petersburg. They had a whole army of young followers, both male and female, but unlike the Populists or the Nihilists, they did not inspire a wider youth movement. And yet, I believe that the poets and artists of the Silver Age did constitute a subculture, a subculture of which they were the only members.

Despite the enormous diversity of the aesthetic tastes of the writers, artists and composers of the time, they all slotted into one cultural niche by setting themselves up in opposition to the traditions of the preceding century. They opposed not only the pompous, semi-official neo-classical culture of Orthodoxy, autocracy and nationalism, but also the revolutionary and democratic tendencies of realist novelists, of the Mighty Handful composers and of artists like The Wanderers. This is not to say that they were centrists; rather, they were true radicals because they adopted an entirely new frame of reference.

But let us start at the beginning. In 1892 a 27-year-old author named Dmitry Merezhkovsky published the collection *Symbols: Songs and Poems*, which was heavily influenced by Dostoevsky, Charles Baudelaire and Edgar Allen Poe. This publication represented the birth of a new movement in Russian literature and culture in general: Symbolism. In that same year, Merezhkovsky also published a sensational article called *The Reasons for the Decline in Contemporary Russian Literature, and New Trends in it* in which he describes Symbolism as a combination of mystical content, symbolic language and impressionistic presentation.

Symbolism was certainly no overnight success: popular acclaim would not come until the second generation of Symbolists like Alexander

Portrait of Zinaida Gippius. Leon Bakst, 1906.
Courtesy of the State Tretyakov Gallery, Moscow

ZINAIDA GIPPIUS
(1869–1945)

Russian literature has had better poets, but very few
more colourful characters than Gippius, the doyenne of
Symbolism who was, in her own words "wounded from
childhood by love and death". Her salon and her open
marriage with writer and philosopher Dmitry Merezhkovsky were at the centre of literary life for nearly 50
years. A bisexual, cross-dressing dandy, Gippius was
an inspiration in her time and beyond.

Blok in the 1900s. At first, readers inclined towards Populism and revolutionary democracy distanced themselves from what seemed like anti-social mumbo-jumbo. Nonetheless, Merezhkovsky was joined by other writers who shared his interest in Oscar Wilde, French poetry and Russian mystical philosopher Vladimir Solovyov. One of the first was Valery Bryusov, who in 1894, at the age of 19, authored a play with the rather telling title: *The Decadents (End of the Century)*. Another was Zinaida Gippius – just a few years older than Bryusov, this charismatic and scandalous young poet not only became Merezhkovsky's wife but also something of an icon of Russian Symbolism. In 1896 she published a book of short stories called *The New People* – a clear reference to the new people of Chernyshevsky's *What Is To Be Done?* Unlike Vera Pavlovna and her friends, however, the heroes of Gippius's stories eschewed both practicality and optimism in favour of mystical portents and individualistic self-development. Above all, the Symbolists rejected what they saw as realism's naïve belief in the possibility of material understanding in favour of creativity based on impressionism, intuition and insight into mystery. "Art is a way of understanding the world in ways that are not rational," proclaimed Bryusov. They were influenced not by Marx, but by Nietzsche: with typical Bolshevik candour, Trotsky alluded to the latter when he criticised the Symbolist worldview as originating in a desire to "Lose oneself, to emerge beyond good and evil".

This alleged desire for oblivion has a lot in common with a second cornerstone of the Silver Age mentality – what I would call 'apocalypse syndrome' – the feeling that in French is associated with the *fin de siècle*. People read signs into everything around them, thinking that they presaged an immediate catastrophe or degradation and annihilation. They saw progress as illusory or vulgar. Human relations were dominated by mutual alienation and immorality. The dismal reality of what was happening in Russia at the time certainly contributed to these feelings of pessimism: an unnecessary war against Japan in 1904-05 turned into a spectacular defeat and the revolutionary events it spawned in the Revolution of 1905 also failed, poisoned by violence. Moreover, when the last of the Russian tsars, Nicholas II had ascended to the throne in 1894, he had brought with him a decadence which, along with his weakness, his indecisiveness and his superstition, combined to provide a perfect picture of an empire in decline.

But the pioneering spirits of the Silver Age had two tools to help them overcome the all-pervading air of depression: a penchant for experimentation and a taste for dandyism. Not only did the Symbolists stand out for the strange, unrealistic, irrational content of their works, but they also made several daring innovations in form. Take Bryusov's famous one-line poem, which prompted an avalanche of ridicule and parodies: "Oh cover your pale legs." It was the Symbolists who made the first steps in the use of provocative imagery, paradoxical metaphors and phonetic

Valery Bryusov under the table,
1900s

play which would become the hallmarks of their poetic successors, the Futurists – of whom more shortly. Of more subcultural importance, however, was the Symbolists' dandyism. It was here that Zinaida Gippius really came into her own – she was indisputably the Russian dandy-dame number one, truly the 'Madonna of decadence'. She possessed in abundance the vivid individualism and desire to shock that was characteristic of the classical dandy. She was the first Russian woman to regularly wear men's clothes. While openly gay poet Mikhail Kuzmin was the most fashion forward of the Symbolist men, judging by portraits, Bryusov, with his charming goatee beard and lush, well groomed moustache, was also no stranger to refinement. It was partly a reaction against this aestheticism – and the Symbolist predilection for airy talk about mysterious realms – that motivated the next phase of the Silver Age, which first manifested itself in the emergence of robust and inventive new styles in painting. In the early years of the 1910s competing groups of young artists with fantastical names like the 'Jack of Diamonds' and the 'Donkey's Tail' held a series of exhibitions in which they showcased their original works. At first these bore witness to the influence of French Post-Impressionism and Cubism, but soon a freewheeling, uniquely Russian style emerged which combined naïve art, folklore motifs and abstract images. It was in these exhibitions that some of the most famous artists of the twentieth century made their debuts, such as Mikhail Larionov, Natalia Goncharova, Kazimir Malevich, Marc Chagall and El Lissitzky. The innovative artists of the avant-garde raced forward, cycling through different styles and often having little in common but their commitment to radical aesthetic change. However, late in 1912 a literary movement surfaced which articulated many of the dominant tendencies of the art of its day. That movement was Futurism.

The first Russian Futurists had originally called themselves the *budetlyane* (from the Russian word *budet* – 'it will be') and it's a great shame that they left this name behind and borrowed the term 'Futurist' from Filippo Tommaso Marinetti's *Manifesto of Futurism* (1909). The Russian Futurists were similar to their Italian namesakes in that they were very young and fierce and completely rejected the past while welcoming the future. The *budetlyane* had in fact published their first collection in 1910, but it was with the scandalous publication of their manifesto *A Slap in the Face of Public Taste* in 1912 that they became household names. In it they set out their virulent rejection of both Symbolism and of the classics.

- We alone are the face of our Time… The past is too tight. The Academy and Pushkin are more incomprehensible than hieroglyphs. Throw Pushkin, Dostoevsky, Tolstoy and so on and so on from the steamship of Modernity.
- Who, naïve, would give his last Love to the perfumed lechery of Balmont? Can we find in that the brave masculine spirit of today? Who, cowardly, is afraid to tear the paper armour from Bryusov's black frock coat? …

Kazimir Malevich's work at The Last Futurist Exhibition of Paintings 0,10 (*Zero Ten*), 1915–16

David Burliuk, 1928

- From the heights of skyscrapers we look down on these
  nonentities.
- We demand that you respect poets' rights:
- To broaden the scope of the poet's vocabulary with fabricated and
  derivative words (word-innovation).
- To despise with all their heart the language that existed before them.
- To wrench the laurel wreath of cheap fame from their proud brow
  with horror – it is made from bath-house switches.
- To stand on the rock of 'we' amidst an ocean of hisses and outrage.

Reading that, the Nihilists would have been proud of their descendants and the punks of the 1970s would laud their radicalism. The manifesto was written in one day in a Moscow hotel room by four young men: Velimir Khlebnikov (27), David Burliuk (30), Alexei Kruchenykh (26) and Vladimir Mayakovsky (19). From it, one can derive the basic tenets of Russian Futurism:

- The cult of the future and the desire to accelerate its arrival.
- The future is seen in the most general of terms but is always bright
  and colourful.
- Rebellion against the present – not so much politically and socially
  as culturally, morally and aesthetically.
- The total rejection of the artistic dogmas and achievements of the
  past as incompatible with the aesthetics of the present and
  especially of the future.
- Radical experimentation with poetic form – rhythm, rhyme,
  punctuation, sound.
- The desire to change the language, inventing new words and
  phrases.

In regard to the last point, two of the Futurists went further than the others: Khlebnikov and Kruchenykh. The latter practically invented his own autonomous language, known as *zaum* or 'beyondsense', which rejected all existing Russian words in favour of a lexicon of his own invention. Without knowing Russian you might not appreciate the strangeness of his most famous poem, but you might capture something of its unusual sonic qualities if i quote it here:

Dyr bul shchyl
ubeshshchur
skum
vy so bu
rlez

Kruchenykh said of his poem: "There is more Russian nationality in these five lines than in all the poetry of Pushkin." When it did use existing Russian words, Futurist poetry exhibited a love for rough, plebeian, 'anti-aesthetic' language and shocking images. Here, for example, are some well-known lines by David Burliuk:

The soul is a pub,
The sky – a rag,
Beauty is blasphemous crap,
And Poetry – a worn-out slag.

The Futurist movement was not monolithic: in addition to the core St Petersburg faction, which included the authors of *A Slap* and which described itself as 'Cubo-Futurist' in a nod to the influence of painting, there was the Moscow grouping Centrifuge, where a 23-year-old Boris Pasternak published his first poems, and the Ego-Futurists, led by Igor Severyanin, a man famous for his extraordinary ego – "I am the genius Igor Severyanin!" and pretentiousness – "Champagne in a lily, champagne in a lily!".

The Futurists, many of whom painted a little, were close to a group of artists known as the 'Union of Youth', which included among their number Pavel Filonov, Marc Chagall and Vladimir Tatlin, as well as Kazimir Malevich, who designed the set for the Futurist opera *Victory Over the Sun* in 1913. The *budetlyane*, with their reckless energy, optimism and modicum of organisational talent soon found themselves at the centre of avant-garde activity.

But the Futurists represented only one strand during this incredibly rich time in Russian culture, when St Petersburg cafés like the famous *Stray Dog* played host to multitudes of young bohemians representing new trends in art and poetry. How I would have loved to be there. If I were asked what five-year period in the history of Russian art was the most important and fruitful, I would say without a shadow of a doubt: 1910–1915.

It is telling that the work which marked the end of this creative carnival of tomorrow today was that most enigmatic of paintings, Malevich's *Black Square*. Initially, the artist had developed the image of a black square while working on the scenery for *Victory Over the Sun*, in which it represented the triumph of human creativity over the symbol of nature, the circle of the sun. Thereafter, there have been many interpretations of this famous image, which has been seen as everything from a prank to 'the end of art'. In any case, one can agree with the Modernist artist Alexandre Benois, who, in his review of the *0.10* exhibition at which the square was first exhibited in December 1915, wrote: "This is without doubt, the icon which our friends the Futurists are offering as a replacement for our Madonnas and shameless Venuses."

The Stray Dog Café, which ran from 1911 to 1915

Portrait of Osip Brik.
Alexander Rodchenko, 1924.
Courtesy of the
Alexander Rodchenko and
Varvara Stepanova archive

Cover for About That
by Vladimir Mayakovsky,
featuring Lilya Brik.
Design by Alexander
Rodchenko, 1923.
Courtesy of the
Alexander Rodchenko and
Varvara Stepanova archive

LEF (1923–1929)

One of the most prominent and influential of the many literary and artistic associations that existed in the relative freedom of the 1920s, LEF (the Left Front of Arts), was founded in 1923 by Vladimir Mayakovsky. It combined a focused aesthetic philosophy, expressed through its flagship magazine, with wide-ranging activity, from poetry to science, in a sincere attempt to invent the culture of the Communist future. This was based on three principles: the rejection of fiction, the embracing of industrial production and the subordinating of creative endeavours to the solving of political and social problems. The end of LEF's second incarnation, 'New LEF', in 1929 was one of the markers of the end of the avant-garde project.

VLADIMIR MAYAKOVSKY (1893–1930)

A poet and provocateur, a dandy and a showman, Mayakovsky has been an icon for many generations of radical Russian artists. He has always come to the fore at times of rapid cultural renewal like Khrushchev's Thaw or Gorbachev's perestroika. A handsome hooligan and committed Futurist, Mayakovsky was a punk rocker before either punk or rock. His dream of a future right here and right now turned into a nightmare when the oppressive bureaucratic machine of Stalinism started mercilessly destroying any chance of a Communist utopia.

I can't say exactly where the Futurists' incredible creative energy came from, what fed their belief in their imminent 'victory over the sun' – an extraordinary utopia that was less artistic than it was civilisational.

The banal explanation: the quick acceleration of capitalism in Russia combined with a weakening monarchy and the resultant head-spinning cognitive dissonance caused by the clash of archaism and progress. Another explanation: the avant-garde carried with it a huge number of excited young people. No single cultural movement in Russia had yet had such a resonance – this really was the rock and roll of its time. Indeed, there were quite a few similarities between the 1910s and the turbulent 1960s, between the Silver Age and the 'Age of Aquarius': a shared spirit of disowning the past, a feeling that the future was just around the corner. By the way, a good dose of morphine and cocaine – then just coming into fashion – helped to catalyse this chemical reaction. But all the while, the future really was sneaking up on the avant-garde, from a most unexpected direction. In August 1914 the First World War began, with Russia as an active participant. The Futurist Benedikt Livshits volunteered for the front. The *Stray Dog* emptied out and when, in 1915, Mayakovsky gave an anti-war speech, the cafe was closed down permanently. 1917 saw the double whammy of two Russian revolutions – the long awaited revolution by the anti-monarchist bourgeoisie in February, and a second, unexpected and unpredictable, revolution at the end of October, led by the Bolsheviks. Summer, it seems, is not the time for revolution in Russia.

As strange as it may seem, the decadent avant-garde beau monde initially reacted to these radical and fateful changes in the country's fortune with perplexity and stoicism, either pretending – or truly believing – that nothing out of the ordinary had taken place. Here is the writer Vladislav Khodasevich's magnificent description of a society event in St Petersburg just two years after the 1917 October Revolution:

"In 1920 there was a ball organised at the Institute of the History of Art at Christmas. I remember miserable lighting and frosty steam in the huge, frost-bound halls of the Zubov mansion in St Isaac's Square. Damp logs moulder and glow in the fireplaces. The entire literary and artistic world of St Petersburg is present. The music is pounding. People are moving around in the half darkness, crowding around the fireplaces. My God, how this crowd is dressed! Felt boots, sweaters and worn fur coats which one can't take off even in the ballroom. And here, with befitting lateness, comes (the poet Nikolai) Gumilyov with a lady in a black low-cut dress on his arm, trembling from the cold. Standing tall and with a haughty air, Gumilyov walks through the rooms in a tailcoat. He shudders from the cold but offers majestic and decorous bows to his right and to his left. He chats to acquaintances in a high-society tone of voice. He plays at being at a ball. His whole look says, 'Nothing has happened. Revolution? Never heard of it.'"

In his 1918 article "Russian Dandies", Alexander Blok, one of a very small number of Symbolists who accepted the Bolshevik' revolution, describes in an angry and bewildered tone his meeting with the 20- year-old poet Valentin Stenich, who described the young decadents' milieu as follows: "All of us are drug friends and opium addicts. Our women are nymphomaniacs. We are a minority but, for the time being, we call the shots among the youth. We mock those who show an interest in socialism, work and the revolution. We live by poetry alone."

Confirming Stenich's words, Blok complains that such "dandies" can even be found among the workers and peasants. Among artists and writers, the majority of whom felt alienated from – or even hostile to – the changes wrought by the Communists, the Futurists stood apart. For them, revolution was just one necessary (and by no means final) step on the path towards the destruction of the dogmatic past and the construction of the utopian world of tomorrow.

To accept or not to accept? There was no such question for me or my fellow Muscovite Futurists, "It is my revolution," wrote Mayakovsky in his autobiography *I Myself*. "I came to Smolny (the Communist headquarters). I began to work." As well as composing revolutionary poems, the Futurists wrote proclamations calling for the democratisation of art. Mayakovsky founded a short-lived literary group called 'Komfut' (short for Communist Futurism) and then, with more success, LEF, the Left Front of Art, a radical avant-garde journal and publishing house, all the while travelling widely in Russia and abroad. Burliuk emigrated to the USA via Japan and

Russian cruiser Aurora. On 25th October 1917 a blank shot from her forecastle gun signaled the start of the assault on the Winter Palace and the beginning of the October Revolution

THE OCTOBER REVOLUTION

In February 1917 Russia, beset by military failure, economic catastrophe and weak leadership, achieved the same thing that had happened in England in the seventeenth century and France at the end of the eighteenth century; a bourgeois revolution and the fall of the monarchy. This was not enough for Lenin, who in his famous *April Theses* called for a proletarian takeover of power. In late October, during a period of relative anarchy, the Bolshevik Revolution – seen by its detractors as a coup – was launched in St Petersburg under the leadership of Leon Trotsky. Alexander Kerensky, head of the Provisional Government fled, disguising himself by wearing a dress. Power was seized by the Bolsheviks and the soviets, representative organisations for workers, peasants and soldiers.

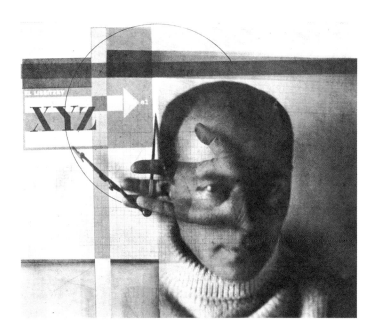

Kruchenykh, the most extreme of the Futurists, settled temporarily in Georgia then back in Moscow, while Khlebnikov, the most enigmatic and perhaps most talented of the Futurists, went to Persia in support of the Red Army, then, on his return, fell ill with typhus and died.

The Russian cultural revolution of the early twentieth century was overtaken by a social revolution. The consequences of this were, to put it mildly, not good. A great many of the figureheads of the Silver Age immediately emigrated – including Gippius and Merezhkovsky, as well as ballet impresario Sergei Diaghilev and the composers Igor Stravinsky and Sergei Rachmaninoff. Some watched the new Soviet regime with interest and even welcomed it, but after a few years of lost illusions also emigrated, like Kandinsky and Burliuk. Others stayed behind, only to die soon after from various causes, like the poets Sergei Yesenin (suicide), Alexander Blok (illness) and Nikolai Gumilyov (execution).

Nevertheless, in the first decade of the Soviet regime, before the Stalinist dictatorship and enforcement of Communist bureaucracy really took hold, experiments in culture and art were permitted and even encouraged. After all, the new socialist art was the art of the future. This period gave us the films of Dziga Vertov, the photographs of Alexander Rodchenko, the posters and collages of El Lissitzky, the constructivist architecture of Vladimir Tatlin and Konstantin Melnikov, the designs of Varvara Stepanova and the industrial music of Alexander Mosolov. Many of the names from this period are still well known in the twenty-first century and sometimes even now I see images of their work on T-shirts and album covers. But in the Soviet Russia of the 1920s they were a dying tribe of romantics, castaways from a new world. They were soon to be replaced by totalitarian baroque, the Stalinist gothic, Socialist Realist literature and classical ballet. In this context, the suicide of onetime Futurist firebrand Vladimir Mayakovsky in 1930 seems like a fairly logical course of action.

Vladimir Tatlin before the Monument to the Third International, 1920. Heritage Images / Getty Images

Anna Akhmatova. Moisei Nappelbaum, 1924

Construction of The monument to the Third International (Tatlin's Tower), 1920

Alexander Rodchenko and Varvara Stepanova, 1923. Courtesy of the Alexander Rodchenko and Varvara Stepanova archive

Pyramid of Women; sports parade on Red Square. Alexander Rodchenko, 1936.
Courtesy of the Alexander Rodchenko and Varvara Stepanova archive

CHAPTER 5

Party Animals: The Komsomol and the Anti-Stalin Underground. 1930–1956

Totalitarian regimes have always dealt pitilessly with political opposition, refusing to permit the development of civil society, crushing any intellectual dissent and censoring freedom-loving culture. Any manifestations of subcultural energy are similarly unwelcome: there is only one leader, one nation, one style, one music. Stalin's regime, in control of the country from the late 1920s, played an evil joke on the avant-garde: by the 1930s, in a new paradigm of politics and bureaucracy, their genuine loyalty to the ideals of the revolution looked silly and even suspicious. Their eccentricity, passion for experimentation and innovation presented a stark contrast to the officially sanctioned conservative doctrine of Socialist Realism. The soviet leadership, whose policies became established by the early 1930s, required the public to be obedient and identical. The instruments used to create this grey mass of humanity were fear and brainwashing.

Young people were designated their own space in the construction of this matrix: they represented the most mobile, and at the same time, the most problematic, section of society. On the one hand, young men and women are more easily influenced, which is good; on the other, they are more susceptible to free-thinking, to frustration and to the dangerous habit of asking unwanted questions. It was with the consolidation of Bolshevik power and the establishment of the USSR in 1922 that, for the first time, Russia acquired a focused youth policy with specific disciplinary and organisational aims. It had three components: loyalty to the party and its leader, hard work and militarism. This system has now been perfected in North Korea, where citizens walk around in uniforms wearing a compulsory badge bearing the image of the leader. As it became more conscious of global opinion, and of common sense, during the last decades of its existence the Soviet Union knew only a lukewarm version of this ideology. But it didn't start out like that. And the organisation that was responsible for constructing and managing the Communist consciousness of young people was the Komsomol. Up until now I have never really thought much about why the Komsomol was created. Why was it necessary? In the USSR, the Komsomol, which is sometimes translated as the Communist Youth League, was a monstrously large government organisation which brought together tens of millions of young Soviets aged from 14 to 28 in its endless ranks. During Soviet rule the Komsomol was so organic and all-pervasive that the question of how it came about and the reason for its existence somehow never arose. One can say the following three things about the Komsomol with certainty:

- It was the biggest youth movement in the history of Russia.
- Having been spawned "from above", it was a purely official organisation (at least from the early 1930s on).
- Since Komsomol members wore identical badges and learned identical texts and songs off by heart, it was very different from the other subcultures in this book – in a way it's a sort of counterexample.

The Bolshevik leaders came to power after the October Revolution in 1917 at a time when they were no longer young – Lenin was 47 and Trotsky 38 – but the vast majority of their followers, the cannon fodder of the revolution and the ensuing civil war, were very young, some of them just teenagers. The popular Soviet writer Arkady Gaidar is a typical example: he joined the ranks of the Red Army and became a member of the Communist Party at the age of 14. He was a Group Commander by 15, but when he was 18 (still a teenager, but now at the rank of colonel), he was expelled from the Party and the Army for using unnecessary cruelty when carrying out a massacre of peaceful civilians in southern Siberia.

This is reminiscent of the actions of the Chinese Red Guards during the Cultural Revolution and the mass executions of city-dwellers in Pol Pot's Cambodia, which were also carried out by soldiers who were not much older than children.

Perhaps the idea of a youth organisation for workers and peasants came about as a way to somehow control and rule these raging masses intoxicated by the winds of change and smell of blood. Initially much of the talk was about creating a political party, but the Bolsheviks wisely decided not to create a competitor, which might have been risky, and instead, in October 1918, created the Russian Communist Youth League. Initially, it consisted of 22,100 members. Two years later it had 482,000 members. It was at this time that the famous Third Komsomol Congress took place, the only one to be addressed by Lenin. His speech, often called "The Tasks of the Youth League", was still being drummed into us in schools over half a century later. Lenin began and ended the speech by saying that it was up to the young generation to build a Communist society and that those who were now 15 years old – and there were quite a few 15-year-old delegates at the Congress – would be lucky enough to live in a Communist state. Which was somewhat optimistic. Lenin said that the main task of young men and women was simple and non-violent: It was to study. To study

VLADIMIR LENIN (1870–1924)

The leader of the Russian Communist Revolution is now somewhat overlooked, after more than half of a century of cultic adoration. A dogmatic Marxist, a professional revolutionary by the age of 23 and a brilliant politician, polemicist, and orator, Lenin was possibly the only true intellectual to lead Russia for many centuries and one of the few to be indifferent to material wealth and personal power. His negative characteristics included political opportunism bordering on cynicism and a fanatic's disregard for the value of human life. Unlike his successor Stalin, however, who is still revered by sadomasochistic Russians today, Lenin never treated bloodshed as a means to an end or a macabre hobby, but rather as an unavoidable byproduct of the dictatorship of the proletariat.

Vladimir Lenin. From the series
Life of Fabulous Monroes.
Vladislav Mamyshev-Monroe,
1996.
Courtesy of the
Aksenov Family Foundation

Communism, as he put it. He even warned young radicals against ignoring the bourgeois science and culture of the old school, citing a phrase which was soon to be plastered across millions of posters: "You can only become a Communist when you have enriched your mind with the knowledge garnered by mankind throughout history."

At the end of the speech, in a response to a question from the audience about the Komsomol's relationship to the Communist Party, Lenin replied simply that the Komsomol would work under the leadership of the Party and carry out its commands. It's interesting to think that we, the young Komsomol members of the 1970s, were never informed of two fundamental facts about the organisation: who the founding members were and who its first chairman was. There was a good reason for this. The Russian Communist Youth League was founded by Lazar Shatskin, who in 1918 was 16, and Oscar Rivkin, who was then 19. Their names clearly betrayed their Jewish origin – something of a problem during later periods of semi-official anti-Semitism. What's more, they were both shot during Stalin's purge of 1937-38. In fact all the leaders of the early Komsomol – all without exception – were arrested at the same time and either perished in the basement of the NKVD (the KGB of the time) headquarters or in the gulag: Nikolai Chaplin, Efim Tsetlin and Pyotr Smorodin. Youngsters like this – passionate, romantic, educated, ambitious – did not fit into the bureaucratic machine of the Stalinist dictatorship and they served as an ideal target for reprisals.

This did not, however, prevent the obedient Komsomol organisation from growing and flourishing. Under the leadership of new chairmen, the young generation eagerly participated in all sorts of Party projects. In the USSR, the Komsomol had no rivals; what few anarchist, revolutionary cells there were had been destroyed in the early 1920s. The scouts were banned in 1922 and replaced by the Communist children's organisations of which I myself was a member – the Octobrists and the Pioneers – where games, trips away and nights huddled around a camp fire all became part of ideological training. The existence of a huge, totally exclusive youth organisation like the Komsomol was a unique experiment in the history of Russia. And, in my opinion, a failed experiment. As we can see from the example of Eastern European countries which had their own versions of the Komsomol, it is virtually impossible to keep young people under one umbrella organisation and instil them with identical tastes and ideas. If it is possible, then only for a very short time. The only times when the Komsomol was not an artificial exercise was in the 1920s when it rallied together a relatively small number of enthusiasts from the ideological vanguard of young Communists and again during the patriotic fervour of the Second World War. In my lifetime the Komsomol saw a resurgence in enthusiasm at the end of the 1950s and beginning of the 1960s because of the relaxation of censorship under Nikita Khrushchev and because of real Soviet achievements such as Sputnik and Gagarin – the subject of the next chapter. That was the time when the best Komsomol songs were composed and they are perhaps the greatest legacy we have from this gigantic project.

Komsomol rhetoric reflected the idealistic, educational character of the organisation. One of the best known slogans was "Study, study and study as the great Lenin taught us!" As children we were all made to repeat the mantra "Pioneer, be an example to every other child!" and poor marks in school were treated as a sign of ideological inferiority as well as laziness. We were often admonished in school with the words "You are a disgrace to the name of the Pioneers!" Political indoctrination in schools was relentless: as I said earlier, this did not sit well with me, resulting in my expulsion from the organisation. Twice. And yet, a year and a half later (in a third school), despite my past behaviour, I was accepted back into the Komsomol! Nobody asked if I wanted to become a member, it was a fait accompli. The year was 1970: it was the hundredth anniversary of Lenin's birth and everyone joined, whoever they were. So now, as a young, anti-Soviet citizen, I had been forced into a shameful compromise with the authorities. I wanted to go to Moscow State University, but I knew that this would be impossible if I were not a Komsomol member.

I can't say that being a member affected me much or made a difference to my way of life. I never really attended the regular meetings or political information sessions – and with no dire consequences. Having received my degree, I simply stopped paying my membership fees and silently slipped away from the Komsomol. By the 1970s this was possible.

The Komsomol had degenerated from an ideologically charged youth organisation of enthusiasts and activists into an amorphous and hypocritical bureaucratic organisation that was nothing more than a docile and dumb appendage of the Communist Party of the Soviet Union. However, the Komsomol still had its uses for the Party: it trained youngsters to be conformist and, more importantly, was a source of an extremely pliable work force. The government would send hundreds of thousands of young Komsomol members on trips to whatever gigantic state project was going on at the time – whether it was the development of new land for farming, the construction of a hydroelectric power plant or the laying of railway tracks in Siberia. Perhaps the only difference between the Komsomol members and the slaves in the gulag was that they had freedom of movement, the right to a private life and a salary. But it was the state which controlled their labour and their professional development. While the Komsomol certainly had an economic raison d'être, I doubt very much whether, by the time I became a member, it had an ideological one. Despite the might of youth propaganda and counter-propaganda (in the 1970s there were 131 Komsomol newspapers with a circulation of 16 million, plus dozens of magazines), the Komsomol was still infected by the capitalist contagion, which we will examine in the next few chapters. If, in the 1950s, Komsomol patrols in the streets looked vaguely like American

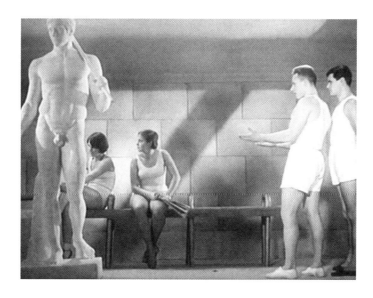

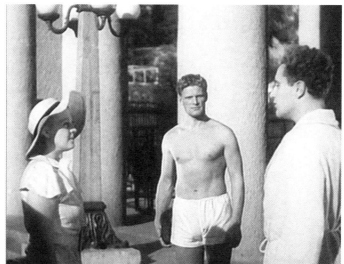

Stills from the film
A Strict Youth
by Abram Room, 1935

hipsters (more of them in the next chapter), then in the 1970s they proudly went out wearing platform boots and jeans, listened to Elton John and smoked Marlboro cigarettes. All aspects of young people's leisure time were controlled by the Komsomol, and it was with the help of Komsomol committees that members managed to hold unofficial rock concerts, festivals, discos and exhibitions. However, if there was a hint that the authorities might get wind of these events, or if some other risk arose, the Komsomol officials quickly put a stop to them because, to them, their careers were more important than some trendy concert. In the Soviet government the Komsomol was considered to be the dumping ground for talentless losers. The most ambitious young officials strove to move on to more serious government departments, such as the Communist Party of the Soviet Union, the KGB, the Ministry of Defence or the Ministry of Foreign Affairs. The attitude to those who chose a career in the Komsomol was one of contempt: not only did these portly, middle-aged men and women look ridiculous in their little red scarves, but they tended to be pompous layabouts. There is one insider story that perfectly illustrates the typical image of a Komsomol official. There was a certain highly placed official in the Komsomol Central Committee who used to spend his days asleep in his office. However, since people would occasionally pop their head round the door, he didn't want to lie down on the sofa to sleep, so instead took his naps sitting at his table with his chin cupped in his hands. However, one day his hands slipped and the poor bureaucrat broke his jaw. If my memory doesn't fail me, not a single significant Komsomol official was promoted on to another government department.

The Komsomol's end came with a whimper rather than a bang. Overcome with inertia, it had started to fall apart in the late 1980s, before the collapse of the Soviet Union. Officially, however, it came to an end in 1991, an event that went completely unnoticed.

The Anti-Stalin Underground

The Komsomol had a sort of mirror image, a shadow which has been all but forgotten – the anti-Stalinist underground. It was made up of young people who were convinced Marxists and Communists but who hated the Stalinist regime, the regime that eventually destroyed them. They had nothing in common with the pompousness and ideological emptiness of the Komsomol. I first read about them in Alexander Solzhenitsyn's *Gulag Archipelago*, where he briefly mentions a group of very young lads, many of them schoolchildren, who distributed anti-Party leaflets and so were sent to the camps in Siberia. Some years later, toward the end of the 1980s, at the peak of the 'glasnost campaign' for openness, the memoirs of writer and poet Anatoly Zhigulin were published under the title *Black Stones*. He describes an underground organisation of schoolchildren

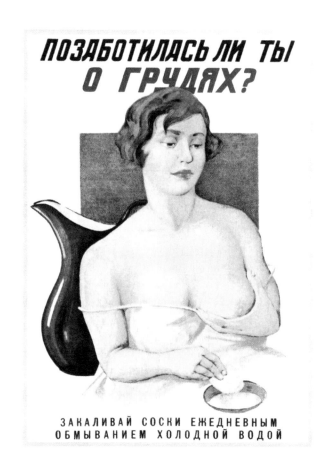

ПОЗАБОТИЛАСЬ ЛИ ТЫ
О ГРУДЯХ?

ЗАКАЛИВАЙ СОСКИ ЕЖЕДНЕВНЫМ
ОБМЫВАНИЕМ ХОЛОДНОЙ ВОДОЙ

ОТ ЖАРКОЙ РАБОТЫ
ТАЕТ ТВОЙ СРОК!

"Your shift is melted away by your hot work!" Canal Army Poster. Dmitlag artist Konstantin Sobolewski, 1936

"Have you taken care of your breasts? Steel your nipples with daily cold sponge baths." Pavel Bekhmetyev, 1930

called the 'Communist Youth Party' (CYP), which was active in Voronezh in 1948 and 1949. It was organised by a group of teenagers in a boys' school and was led by a lad called Boris Batuev, the son of a local Party leader. In the two years of its existence, the CYP managed, in great secrecy, to gather together around 60 youngsters of the same age. Their party manifesto proclaimed that they would follow the ideas of Lenin and fight for the overthrow of the Stalinist regime. In the autumn of 1949, just as these young communists were graduating from school, the majority of them were arrested, interrogated, tortured, tried and sent to the gulag.

At about the same age as these boys I was plagued by this question: how could the people of the USSR just sit back and silently tolerate the Stalinist terror? Why did they not revolt? Why had no one put an end to the sadistic tyrant? Well, as *Black Stones* showed me, there was some resistance, but its existence was heavily suppressed both during and after the Soviet Union.

In the early years of the Soviet Union, although the Bolsheviks' direct rivals such as the anarchists had been eradicated, the concept of 'dissident Marxists' did not exist as such, for the simple reason that the nature of the Party was still being debated even at the highest level. But as the Party, under the strict rule of Stalin, became increasingly monolithic, these discussions were silenced and the representatives of

СОВЕТСКИЕ ФИЗКУЛЬТУРНИКИ—ГОРДОСТЬ НАШЕЙ СТРАНЫ.
За здоровое, жизнерадостное поколение, готовое к труду и обороне социалистической родины!

*"Soviet sportsmen are the country's pride. To a healthy and merry generation,
ready to work and defend its socialist motherland!"* Victor Koretsekiy, 1935

The gulag system, that giant mechanism for destruction and degradation, did not contain death camps like Auschwitz, but rather simply made it much easier to die than to survive. Male and female prisoners worked themselves beyond the point of exhaustion as slave labour on construction sites or in mines, pointlessly breaking rocks and moving earth. Real criminals – thieves, gangsters, murderers – formed a sort of elite minority in the camps , while the majority of those who lived and died were ordinary Soviet people, condemned by denunciations or a careless, overheard word, or for having the wrong parents, or very often, just to make up the numbers.

Osip Mandelstam, 1934. Photograph taken shortly after his arrest

Vsevolod Meyerhold, 1939. Photograph taken shortly after his arrest

different Bolshevik factions were sent away, either behind the barbed-wire fences of Siberia or to an early grave. By the end of the 1930s the Communist Party had established total unquestioning unanimity on policy. It was around this time, around 1940, that we see the emergence of the first notable anti-Stalinist youth organisation: it was called the 'True Communists' and its members were 16-year-olds from Jalal-Abad in the Kyrgyz Republic. The organisation lasted for only a few months, until the leaders of the group, Ivan Yatsuk and Yuri Shokk, began to hand out pamphlets. They were both sentenced to ten years in prison. The remaining three True Communists were given from six to eight years. We know nothing more about them. The verdict at the trial was: "The accused organised a counter-revolutionary group in October 1940 called the 'True Communists' whose aim was to oppose the Party and the Soviet state. This group of young people, who are clearly in a morally fragile state of mind, became involved in reading anti-Soviet literature, and spreading their propaganda among the people by handing out counter-revolutionary pamphlets." The words 'counter-revolutionary' and 'anti-Soviet' are not really valid in this context. On the contrary, the True Communists and all the other left-wing youth organisations actually believed that it was Stalin's policies that were counter-revolutionary; and they had good reason to think so. It was their fundamental belief that Lenin's theories had been betrayed, including the withering away of the machinery of the state; that the principles of democracy, such as free elections to the soviets, had been forgotten; that the Party and society had become too bureaucratic; and that proletarian internationalism had been abandoned in favour of superpower chauvinism. In many ways these accusations dovetailed with Trotsky's ideas, but these young communists reviled the odious name of Trotsky. As far as I know, they didn't question Stalin's reign of terror, or the execution of leaders of the revolution like Trotsky, Nikolai Bukharin and Grigory Zinoviev. On the whole, the True Communists in Kyrgyz Republic and their successors were normal, well-mannered Soviet youngsters. They differed from the silent majority in that they fervently believed in Communist theory and, thanks to a critical frame of mind, were able to see how very far removed this was from Stalin's policies.

On a purely emotional level, their actions and conspiracies could be seen as a continuation of a game called 'Bolshevik Conspirators' we used to play as Pioneers. It's hard to say exactly where the young lads in the far-off Central Asian town of Jalal Abad thought their campaigning would lead them, but the spirit of revolutionary romanticism burning inside them meant they probably didn't even ask that question.

Immediately after the Second World War the atmosphere in the USSR was interesting to say the least. Having been crushed by the Terror of the 1930s, the people returned home flushed with the success of victory. Despite the hardships of the post-war devastation, the mood in the country was upbeat and buoyant with self-esteem. Everyone, especially those who had fought at the front, were well aware that it was not Stalin and the Party leaders who had beaten Hitler, but the ordinary Soviet people. The attitude to the state was now less fearful and obsequious and people looked on Soviet reality with a more critical eye. To some extent it was a repeat of the syndrome of 1812–15 when the Russian army returned victorious from the war in Europe and brought with it a spirit of freedom and a vague desire for change. Stalin and the Party elite were extremely concerned by this mood, and in 1948 began to frenziedly batten down the hatches. A 'campaign against cosmopolitanism' was launched. Its intention was to erase the memory of the alliance with Britain and the United States and, by stirring up anti-Semitism, to incite people's hatred against a new, although familiar, 'internal enemy' – the Jews. These years from 1948 up until Stalin's death in 1953, were marked by a surprising surge in anti-Stalinism among young people. Suzanna Pechuro and Viktor Bulgakov, former members of two underground Moscow organisations, described it as follows: "Young people started creating underground movements as naturally and as eagerly as, in the past, they had joined the ranks of the Komsomol or rushed to Spain (during the Spanish Civil War) or to the front. The people in these underground organisations were usually senior school pupils or young college students. The tasks they set for themselves do not, as a rule, tally with what was actually possible – they wanted nothing less than a complete change in national policy. They never managed to follow through on their plans; it rarely got further than deciding on the organising principles, discussing the programme and very occasionally distributing pamphlets. It was not long before they were arrested, brutally interrogated and punished."

This short quotation summarises the tragic fate of every single underground group. Unfortunately we now know little more about them than their names: the 'Communist Youth Party' in Voronezh, the 'Union for Struggle for Revolution', the 'Society for Freedom and Truth' and the 'Army of the Revolution' in Moscow; the 'Knights of Success' in Moscow and Kharkov; the 'All-Russian Democratic Union' in Moscow and Voronezh; the 'Young Leninists', the 'Young Communists', the 'Young Guard', the 'Lenin Guard'.

There was even an 'All-Union Party against Stalin' in Ulyanovsk, Lenin's hometown. There were cells in Leningrad, Kazan, Tbilisi, Chelyabinsk and other cities across the Soviet Union.

All of these underground 'parties' existed only briefly and were discovered and repressed not so much because of the efficiency of the machinery of state security, but because the custom of denouncing people had, in the 1930s, become the accepted norm in Soviet society. The youngest conspirators, who were still in school at the time, were sometimes given juvenile sentences of between three and four years in prison. However, as a rule, the punishments tended to be between 10–25 years years in a labour camp or even execution. Suzanna Pechuro, who

In reality, Russia's war had started two years earlier in 1939 with the Molotov-Ribbentrop Pact, military aggression in Poland and the attack on Finland, but in Russia people don't like to talk about that. The war had terrible consequences: by its end, 30 million Soviet citizens had died and nearly all the men of the first post-revolutionary generation had perished. Despite these unimaginable sacrifices, the war and especially the ultimate victory have been transformed from a tragedy into a patriotic fetish and symbol for the supposed superiority and invincibility of Russia, first in the post-war USSR, but especially now under Putin.

Suzanna Pechuro. Dubravlag, 1955. From the private archive of Alexey Makarov

Suzanna Pechuro preparing for exams after her release, 1956. From the private archive of Alexey Makarov

was only 17 years old when she was sentenced to 25 years in a labour camp, recalls an incident involving a group of teenage boys from the Society for Freedom and Truth: "The boys carried themselves bravely". On being taken to their communal cell, they asked the other inmates: "Are any of you teachers? Can any of you give us lessons, because we're not going to school now…" The harshest punishment, however, was meted out to the Union for Struggle for Revolution, which existed for only a few short months but was allegedly intending to assassinate one of Stalin's top henchmen, Georgy Malenkov. In 1952 its three leaders, Boris Slutsky, Yevgeny Gurevich and Vladlen Furman, all in their first year at university, were shot. Young Russian radicals traditionally lean towards terrorism, even if it is only theoretical, and we again see that these youngsters were pushed in that direction by a hopeless situation. According to Mikhail Zarayev, one of the members of the Union for Struggle: "Any opposition activity suffered a ruthless crackdown and there was no legal way to appeal to broad sections of the people. At the same time, a handful of 'leaders', headed by Stalin, were playing a disproportionately important role in politics. The forcible removal of these figures, especially the Soviet dictator himself, would have significantly destabilised the bureaucratic regime."

In March 1953 the dictator died a natural death – too late for many of those who opposed him – and the regime did indeed undergo a great transformation. Three years later, almost all the teenagers who had formed underground cells and managed to survive their time in the camps were released.

But still no one was in any hurry to talk about these anti-Stalinist groups, which raised too many awkward questions for Stalin's successors and former colleagues. During the short Khrushchev Thaw, young opposition activists, including those who held Communist beliefs, were all still considered dissidents. And Trotskyites to boot, as many aspects of the system that they had criticised – rigged elections, the lack of real democracy, the dictatorship of bureaucracy, the gap between the party elite and the people and so on – were still true of post-Stalinist political life in the Soviet Union. The arrested and executed heroes and heroines of the anti-Stalinist underground were not exonerated until the late 1980s. But even then, and even after the fall of the regime, these subversives did not receive much recognition; none of these wonderful young men and women went on to become prominent political or cultural figures, although some of them did join the human rights organisation 'Memorial'.

The classic Soviet dissidents and talking heads of the Yeltsin era were mostly anti-Communist, and so these left-wing figures were treated as alien, unsympathetic interlopers who spoiled the glossy image of heroic liberals fighting against the bestial Communists.

In a way, the efforts of the anti-Stalinist left were fruitless for their descendants and the question of their place in Russian history is a

Daniil Kharms,
1931, 1931, 1941.
Photographs of Daniil Kharms from his secret police file: in 1931 before and during his first arrest and in 1941 – being arrested again.

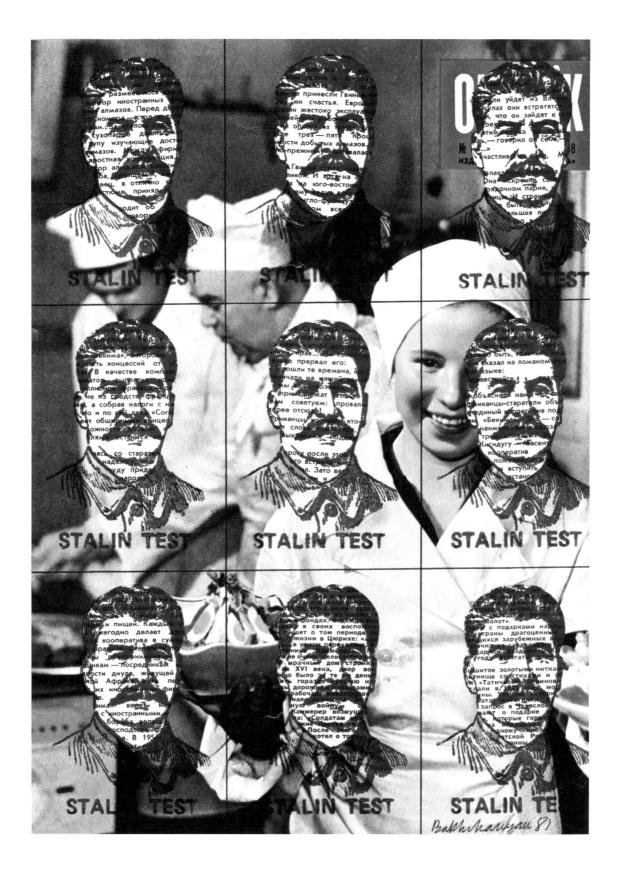

From the series "Stalin Test". Vagrich Bakhchanyan, 1981. Courtesy of the pop/off/art gallery, Moscow

controversial one. Benjamin Joffe, one of the very few people who has properly researched the anti-Stalinist underground movement, claimed that it had "an underlying effect on life in the USSR". Others argue that this 'children's' underground movement was too fleeting and feeble to have any real influence. However, this in no way undermines the personal feats of courage performed by these desperate young people; all it does is make their sacrifice more tragic. With that in mind, I shudder to tell you about the revival of Stalinism and Communist slogans we are seeing in Russia today. It is for that reason that I am doubly glad that I have the opportunity to tell you something about those schoolchildren and students who were unlucky enough to live in that most terrible and bloody period of Russian history, but who were not afraid to think and to act. We must never forget them.

> Do you remember, my friend, our heated arguments?
> How we vowed to find happiness for the people!
> And who would have thought that for this we were doomed
> To end our lives in captivity?
> Fight for Victory, is our glorious cry!
> Fight for Victory! Those sacred words.
> You and I were born in 1930,
> And only began to live in 1949!

> Anatoly Zhigulin, January 1950,
> a poem written in Cell no. 2, the Ministry of State Security Prison.

"All morning I prayed to God that the rain wouldn't ruin my sign."

On the sign: Karl Marx, Friedrich Engels, Vladimir Lenin

Drawings from A Chronicle of Resistance. Victoria Lomasko, 2011–12. Courtesy of the artist

Reproduction of Toadstools by Kukryniksy. Yuri Ivanov, 1967. Courtesy of Sputnik

CHAPTER 6

Heretics and Pagans I: *Stilyagi*, the Black Market and the Soviet Sixties

In his play *Rock 'n' Roll*, set in totalitarian Czechoslovakia in the 1970s, Tom Stoppard makes a beautiful distinction between two very different and mutually hostile types of young people. The first group is the anti-Communist dissidents and human rights activists. Stoppard calls them "heretics". They stand in picket lines, write letters of protest, hand out leaflets and get followed by the secret police. The second group is the "pagans". They are the hippies and rock and roll fans – apolitical and antisocial, they live their own autonomous life outside of the system. Stoppard's question is: which of these two groups is more of a threat to the authorities? You might think that it's obviously the heretics – after all, they're the ones actually opposing the regime. But, through the words of the main hero, Stoppard gives us a strong counter-argument: that's true, he says, but the heretics are playing the same game as the authorities, they speak the same language. The more heretics there are, the bigger and more justified the secret police gets. The pagans, on the other hand, are a black hole for the totalitarian system, their religion is a complete mystery and so they are very difficult to combat. So who exactly poses the bigger threat to the foundation of Communism?

The Soviet youth scene after the Second World War illustrates the situation with the heretics and pagans perfectly. The anti-Stalin underground had been true heretics within the official church – ardent keepers of Communist traditions. But thereafter there were two parallel traditions of resistance to power in the Soviet Union: the dissident heretics, who took on the authorities at their own game, and the pagans – the jazz freaks, the hippies, the rockers – who embraced Western music and culture and turned their backs on Soviet reality almost entirely. The next two chapters will disrupt the chronology of our story slightly in order to trace the parallel development of these two different forms of resistance.

Stilyagi

The grandfathers of all Western-oriented, music-loving subcultures in the Soviet Union were the so-called *stilyagi*, from the word 'style', snappy dressers who took no interest in politics at all. These young men and women just wanted to dance till they dropped – and to music which was not Russian. Ironically, their subculture, which overlapped with the heroic anti-Stalin underground, was, quite unwittingly, far more influential and durable and thus far more dangerous to the Soviet system.

Strange as it may seem, the carefree *stilyagi* and the sincere anti-Stalinists were both spurred on by the same thing – the winds of freedom and independence sweeping the country in the first years after the war. As millions of soldiers returned from the front in the east and the west, the USSR was inundated with foreign goods, including clothes, gramophones and magazines. Exhausted by the war and inspired by their victory, people joyfully danced to the foreign beat of jazz orchestras and stood in line for American films like *Sun Valley Serenade* and *Let George Do It*, or the *German Girl of My Dreams*, which had been taken back to Russia as a trophy of war.

And then it all ended overnight! The Iron Curtain descended and the Cold War began. This new geopolitical turn manifested itself in the daily life of the cities of the Soviet Union as the so-called 'struggle against cosmopolitanism'. Anything foreign was strictly forbidden. Foreign films and music were denounced as an American plot to undermine the Soviet Union. Jazz, tango and the foxtrot were outlawed. It reached the point of total absurdity: the saxophone was condemned as a 'bourgeois instrument' and had to be handed over before entering a building, like a weapon. Some of the wilier musicians managed to straighten out their saxophones and pass them off as clarinets. As usual, most people obediently put their heads down under the blows of yet another dictatorship. But some young people refused to stop the party.

The following long quote is from "Stilyaga", a satirical article published in Soviet humour magazine *Crocodile* in March 1949:

"A literary evening was being held at a student club. After the talk, the dancing was about to begin when a young man appeared in the doorway of the hall. He really looked ridiculous: the back of his jacket was bright orange but the sleeves and the front were green. He wore baggy pea-green-and-canary-yellow trousers the like of which I have never seen before. His boots were a clever combination of black lacquer and red suede. The young man leaned against the door and in a very casual movement he kicked his right leg to the left, displaying socks which looked as if they had been made from bits of the American flag, they were that bright. He stood there and surveyed the room with contemptuously narrowed eyes. "Oh, hello there, Stilyaga! Why were you late for the talk?" asked someone from our crowd. "What a strange young man," I said to the student sitting next to me. "And his name is strange too, I've never heard the surname Stilyaga before." My neighbour laughed. "That's not a surname. A *stilyaga* is a slang name these guys have for themselves. They've developed their own special style, you see, in how they dress, how they talk and how they behave. The key thing about their 'style' is that it doesn't suit ordinary people."

In fact, this indignant, sarcastic text actually contributed considerably to the growth of this new subculture that survived not only the Forties and Fifties but the entire duration of the Soviet Union. The word *stilyaga* was probably not actually coined by the author, as some people think, but after this publication the word soon became so widespread that it served as a general term for thousands of young citizens who wanted to set themselves apart from "ordinary people". The first *stilyagi* appeared in 1947-48 and were easy to identify. Unlike members of the underground, they were not conspiratorial; on the contrary, they were happy to demonstrate their individuality in any way they could and especially in three very innocent things – music, dancing and clothes.

The unofficial soundtrack of the *stilyagi* movement came from American swing music and the orchestras of Glenn Miller, Duke Ellington and Count Basie. Glenn Miller's *Chattanooga Choo Choo,* from *Sun Valley Serenade*, was their theme song. According to scholars, this song about the train leaving Chattanooga was symbolic of the *stilyagi's* distant

Signs of difference. Cover of the Crocodile magazine. Genrikh Valk, 1969.
Courtesy of the Archive of Soviet Caricature and the Russian Blues corporation

Visiting her daughter.

"What are you doing, Mum, that's a portrait of your son-in-law."
Ivan Semenov, 1974

A stilyaga escaping from Sakhalin. Evgeny Shukaev. 1970s

All pictures are courtesy of the Archive of Soviet Caricature and the Russian Blues corporation

"Where is he now, the strong young fellow,
Where is she now, the maiden fair?"
Valery Mokhov, Vladimir Mochalov, 1974

dreamland – America, a mystical place then entirely out of reach of Soviet citizens. I'm not sure that it was all quite as profound as this. The *stilyagi* also enjoyed the foxtrots and tangos that had been popular before the war but forbidden in the 1940s. Much of this music was brought over on records taken from occupied Germany.

Dancing was the *stilyagi's* favourite pastime. They danced in their homes, in restaurants, in cafés and in student clubs. Their dances of choice included the 'Canadian', the 'Atomic' and the 'Triple Hamburg'. American dances, like the boogie-boogie, jitterbug and lindy hop were also popular. It was at the end of the 1950s, at the height of the *stilyagi* phenomenon, that rock and roll made its first appearance. This must have presented a problem: all the rock and roll dances were for couples and among the *stilyagi* there were, by all accounts, more than twice as many boys than girls.

Clothes and hairstyles were as important for the *stilyagi* as they had been for the dandies. The original *stilyagi* looked a lot like the young man in *Crocodile*. Their trousers were wide and short and matched with wool jackets – a 'sporty style'. It was very fashionable to wear knitted sweaters with deers on them in homage to *Sun Valley Serenade*. However, the look changed radically at the peak of the movement, becoming very similar to that of the 'English Teddy Boys': long, bright jackets, usually striped or checked and short, narrow trousers. They wore shoes with thick rubber soles and long, multi-coloured ties. Hawaiian shirts were also popular, along with exotic tiki accessories. Their hair, as with the Teddy Boys, was done up in a quiff with a clearly defined parting and a thin moustache. Their colourful, eye-catching outfits presented a total contrast with the clothes of ordinary Soviet people, which were always grey, black or dark blue. But the *stilyagi's* final and most important accessory was their attitude.

Looking at the many caricatures of *stilyagi* drawn at the time, one is immediately struck by two things. First, the *stilyaga* has his head thrown arrogantly back and looks round at everyone in the room superciliously. Second, he has a rather mincing gait, something between dancing and a catwalk strut. Alexei Kozlov, a well-known saxophonist and former *stilyaga*, writes: "We *stilyagi* had this well-practised empty look about us. Not because we were idiots. It's just that if we showed people what we were really feeling, everyone would see that we hated them. We would have paid dearly for that." I should explain that "they" here means the simple, Soviet people in the street – what the *stilyagi* called *zhloby* ('goons' or 'yobs').

In order to minimise their contact with the alien world of grey, uninteresting people, the *stilyagi* got together in groups. They went to dances and, in winter, to skating rinks (which also played pretty good music); all year round they would meet on 'Broadway'. This was the slang term for the main street in any city: in Moscow it was Gorky Street; in Leningrad, Nevsky Prospect. The *stilyagi* would saunter down Broadway, making new friends, exchanging news and showing off their outfits. But if you took one wrong step, you'd be rubbing shoulders with the *zhloby*. Vladimir Kozlov divides the *stilyagi* into three groups:

The 'Gilded Youth': children of members of the Communist Party or the cultural and diplomatic elite. They were "untouchable" – they had access to the forbidden fruit of foreign records, magazines and albums. They had spacious flats and so were always organising private parties.

The 'Dudes' *(chuvaki)*: true *stilyagi*, lovers of music and Western chic. They were usually the children of middle-class intelligentsia families, but some came from working-class families too. Kozlov singles out certain "hardcore dudes": these *stilyagi* were obsessed not just with jazz but with anything forbidden at the time, from Dostoevsky to abstract art. They despised the Soviet system.

The 'fops' *(pizhony)*: these were just fashionable guys without any convictions. In Kozlov's words, "They didn't care who was in power – as long as they could pick up *stilyagi* chicks, and hang out. They didn't take many risks."

Without a doubt, the *stilyagi* phenomenon was another chapter in the saga of the Russian dandy, although they were probably unaware of this heritage themselves. All the principal attributes of dandyism were in evidence: flamboyance, an ability to stand out against a generic grey background; an exalted, independent attitude; a focus on 'progressive' trends from the West, with particular attention paid to 'style'. But there were some new characteristics too. First, the most obvious one: music and dancing, which had never before been important subcultural elements in Russia, unless we count Populist songs and revolutionary hymns. Second, the post-war Soviet dandy had a totally different social and cultural status. The early nineteenth century dandies, both in Russia and Europe, were highly respected members of the highest echelons of society. Occasionally they even made brilliant careers for themselves, regardless of their extravagant manners. The Russian dandies of the Silver Age, despite their aesthetic revolts and thirst for scandal, were the true trend-setters of their day and age: they were written about, imitated, adored by their benefactors and by the entire progressive elite. The *stilyagi*, for their part, were real dandy-misfits: categorically cast out of the official narrative; the 'healthy majority' of Soviet society, and especially the Komsomol, looked upon them with disdain and mockery.

It would be wrong, in my opinion, to exaggerate the degree of risk the *stilyagi* faced, or to see them as heroes of anti-Communist resistance. Even under Stalin young people were not arrested for ill-advised dances or bright jackets. Nevertheless, the authorities did disapprove of the *stilyagi* – as any totalitarian state would disapprove of those who think differently. The newspapers and magazines of the 1950s were full of anti-*stilyagi* propaganda, from mocking rhymes –

"Every evening George and Fifi go,
    To boogie-woogie dances:
    With every awful shape they throw,
    Bourgeois fashion advances" –

to ideological proclamations – "The *stilyagi* are the epigones of bourgeois aestheticism and have shamed themselves before the people; they carry with them a rootless cosmopolitanism which is profoundly repugnant and entirely hostile to the Soviet people". In practice, there are famous cases when 'hardcore' *stilyagi* were excluded from the Komsomol and expelled from educational establishments, but this wasn't common. A popular method of rounding up the *stilyagi*, still remembered to this day, was to send out 'people's volunteer groups' to catch them. These groups were created at the beginning of the 1950s by keen young Komsomol members in order to maintain order and public morality on the streets of Soviet cities. The volunteers would catch them on the street or in a park and chop off their hair, twist their arms, and use scissors to cut their trousers – which were considered too narrow – at the ankle.

The *stilyagi* still had good fun and lots of adventures, but in 1957 they were dealt a fatal blow. That was the summer when the USSR first opened its borders to the West by staging the World Festival of Youth and Students in Moscow. For the first time in decades, Russia saw an influx of young people from abroad, including Americans. For the *stilyagi*, this was both a dream come true and the end of their illusions. It turned out that, with their bright parrot costumes, their foxtrots and their big-band rhythms, they were actually lagging behind real Western fashion by at least a decade. In a recent Russian movie about *stilyagi*, called *Hipsters* in English (I recommend it, by the way), a young man going back to the USA says to his Moscow friend, a *stilyaga*: "We don't have any *stilyagi* in America!" His friend is shocked, but proudly replies: "But we do here!" Nevertheless, by the end of the 1950s, there were virtually no *stilyagi* left in the USSR either.

One might say that the *stilyagi* were victorious in the end because they did have an effect on the Soviet regime: Khrushchev himself announced at a plenum of the Communist Party that it was high time the Soviet textile industry mastered the production of tight trousers – particularly as this would save on fabric. The head of the KGB, Alexander Shelepin, even made the famous announcement that "a Komsomol member has the right to wear tight trousers!" All the young people in Russia seemed to be dressing in an annoying copy-cat style, so the real *stilyagi* got fed up. The Gilded Youth and the fops found new styles and pastimes. The hardcore dudes split into two warring factions: the 'Yankees' *(shtatniki)* and the 'beatniks'. The Yankees remained true to jazz, but also took an interest in the trendier bebop. They wore double-breasted jackets, long coats and felt hats. The beatniks kept the faith with dancing, but now it was rock and roll and they dressed in blue jeans and black turtlenecks.

Nikita Khrushchev addresses the United Nations, October 1960. Photo by Pat Candido / NY. Daily News Archive via Getty Images

YURI GAGARIN AND
THE SPACE PROGRAMME

Russia's greatest contribution to modern civilisation was probably the breakthrough in space exploration that occurred in the 1950s and 1960s. Led by genius engineer Sergei Korolev, who had been sentenced to the gulag under Stalin, the Soviet space programme launched the first satellite,

Sputnik, in October 1957 and the first live animal, the dog Laika, a month later. The crowning triumph, of course, came in 1961 with the successful spaceflight of Yuri Gagarin at the age of 27. The handsome, smiling Gagarin is probably the only Russian who we can be confident will be remembered forever.

Manchester residents greeting Yuri Gagarin, July 11, 1961.
Photograph:
TASS / Alexei Stuzhin.
Courtesy of ITAR-TASS / Archive

Postage stamp featuring Sputnik, 1957

Both groups were too small to attract the attention of the satirists at *Crocodile*. As we will see below, by then most young people were starting to get excited about a very Soviet chic – Sputnik had been launched and the Soviet Union was about to overtake America in everything.

The *stilyagi* were probably the most charming of all the Russian subcultures of the twentieth century. They weren't a unique phenomenon, however: the famous German swing kids of the 1930s listened to the same music in the face of totalitarian persecution. The *stilyagi* also remind me of the early gay disco scene in America: living on the fringes and putting their all into dancing and dressing up. But for Russia the *stilyagi* were important because they were trailblazers and because they left behind a sense that it was possible to have fun even in the darkest times. If they could do that back then, why should we be discouraged today? Some of their slang – a mix of English words and Jewish musical jargon – still remains current, and they built up a unique underground industry, producing gramophone records on the vinyl from X-rays, which they nicknamed 'discs on bones' or 'babushkas' skeletons'. That aside, I'm afraid they left little for posterity – no literature, no paintings and not even any music of their own. You can't help but agree with the critics who accuse the *stilyagi* of being nothing better than copycats. Their entire culture was borrowed from somewhere else.

In theory, my parents, born in 1928, could have become first-wave *stilyagi*, but they didn't. They studied in the department of history in Moscow State University and did not like dancing. When I was writing my book on rock music I asked my parents what they thought of the *stilyagi*. My father said, "I wasn't interested in them, I never even saw them." My mother added that they looked down on them. When I asked why, she said: "We considered them to be non-entities. They were only interested in fashion and dancing. What about literature, philosophy and politics?" Strangely enough, my parents' viewpoint was similar to that of the authorities and I have some sympathy with it. But I know for sure that, had I been born at that time, I would definitely have been a *stilyaga*. "Freedom, music, clothes!" And actually, they weren't non-entities at all: many of those guys went on to become great writers, poets, actors and musicians. Just not politicians.

The Black Market

Despite not producing much that was their own, the *stilyagi*, with their penchant for Western goods and smuggled records, left Russia one very important material legacy: the black market. This institution soon developed a vibrant subculture all of its own, one that prospered right up to the collapse of the Soviet Union. It's worth departing from our chronology here to examine it in a bit more detail, especially as it played a vital role in all the other subcultures of the period.

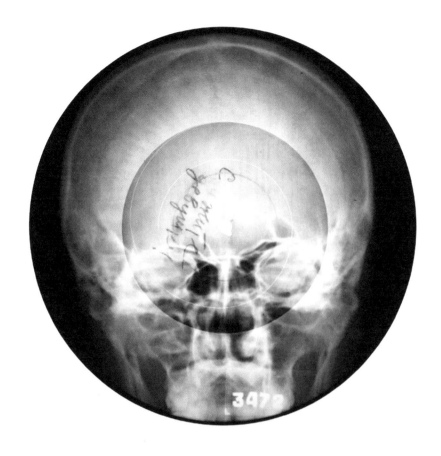

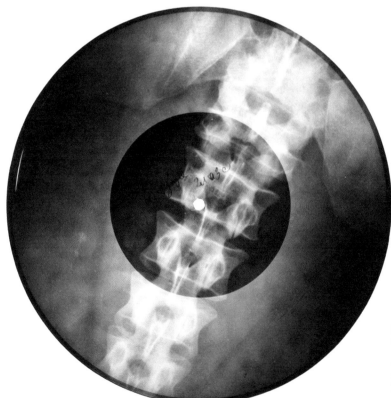

Skull: song "Tell me girls"
Spine: song "Black Eyes"

"Recordings on X-ray film" or
"Music on the Bone".
Late 1940s–50s.
Courtesy of X-Ray Audio Project

It is thought by some that the Russian slang for a black marketeer – 'fartsovshchik' – comes from the English 'for sale'. I doubt that. The first black marketeers didn't buy or sell anything: they just tried to swap interesting things like clothes, magazines and records with the very few foreigners that were in the USSR at that time. But by the end of the 1950s this culture of swapping goods had taken on a very different character and scale. The dress code of the young Soviets became much more liberal: the majority of them, if not all of them, dressed in a style you might call *stilyaga*-light. The country was opening up a little, which meant more foreigners – tourists, students and businessmen. Demand exceeded supply and a small private industry grew up in which black marketeers bought trendy things from foreigners and sold them at a big mark-up to other Russians.

The *fartsovshchiki* inherited some of the characteristics of the *stilyagi*: they dressed well, looked good, spoke the basics of foreign languages and knew something about Western culture – mostly the names of pop stars and popular brands. They were a subculture of sorts – but one with a very clear commercial basis. They were entrepreneurial, and unusually, even obsessively, sociable. Their work had two stages. The first was the riskiest: it was called 'ironing out the firm', which basically meant obtaining quality goods from visitors. They would approach foreigners aggressively in their hotels, by tourist coaches, in bars and even in museums. In exchange for their goods the tourists were offered cameras, Russian souvenirs, furs, vodka and caviar, and sometimes simply Soviet roubles – not at the official exchange rate of course, but at a much higher one. The second stage was selling their plunder on the black market; not, of course, an actual market with stalls, but through dealers, friends, and occasionally even thrift shops.

Whom they targeted depended on the region. In the port towns of the Baltic, Riga and Tallinn, they homed in on foreign sailors; in Leningrad it was Finnish tourists, coming to the town for wild weekends away from tough licensing laws; in Moscow it was diplomats, journalists and businessmen. Black marketeers established long-term relationships with many foreigners – especially the students who studied in the Soviet Union – and put in orders for things well beyond the ordinary tourist range, like electronics and LPs. I myself was pretty active in the black market for music and I can tell you that the volume of records smuggled into the country was pretty impressive. I knew of several apartments in Moscow that looked like proper record shops, and with an enviable selection too.

In the 1970s, at the height of the golden era of the black market, the authorities tried to combat it using the Beryozka chain of shops, which sold rare goods in exchange for foreign currency. But this only served to prompt an even more criminal, and even more risky, enterprise on the part of the *fartsovshchiki* – the buying and selling of US dollars.

A 'check' of Vneshposyltorg, a kind of parallel currency in the USSR used to pay for goods bought in special 'Beryozka' shops selling mostly Western-made goods. 3 rubles, 1976

Beryozka shop, 'Magnolia' hotel in Sochi, Russia, 1970s

Danger lurked everywhere for black market traders, but the most dangerous moment of all was their first approach to foreigners. Their profession was illegal and defined in the Soviet criminal code as 'speculation'. As a rule, when *fartsovshchiki* were caught by KGB officers, police or hotel security, they were released. But not just like that. KGB officers secured the promise that the *fartsovshchik* would join their army of informers and the police took bribes. The attitude of the security forces was just as cynical when it came to the business of the *putany* (foreign currency prostitutes). They worked in hotels and received payment from foreign clients in foreign currency; the sentence for this crime was up to seventeen years in prison, so these women were extremely vulnerable. As well as being obliged to share their earnings with hotel security, they regularly had to report on foreigners to the KGB and were occasionally required to place clients in a 'compromising position'. It is hardly surprising that, in the most famous trial of black market currency dealers in 1960, it turned out that two of the three accused were KGB informants.

The bloody story of this trial deserves a separate mention as it was the first, and last, time in history that the black market was discussed at the highest level of government. Some American 'friends of the USSR' apparently complained to the Deputy Prime Minister, Anastas Mikoyan after they were set upon by some stylish young men outside the Hotel National and offered a very attractive exchange rate for their dollars. Not long afterwards, during a public interview with Nikita Khrushchev in West Berlin, a journalist, in reply to the Soviet leader's criticism of "Berlin speculators", snidely remarked that Moscow had the biggest black market in Europe. What really enraged Khrushchev was not so much the existence

For Soviet women, *Chanel No. 5* was one of the most desirable symbols of the 'bourgeois' west

US citizen charged with unlawful foreign currency transactions and theft of artworks gives evidence during his court hearing. Leningrad, 1960s. Courtesy of The Russian State Documentary Film and Photo Archive, Krasnogorsk

of a black market that undermined the economy, but the implication that people preferred Western products to Soviet ones. Upon his return, he immediately demanded a report on the fight against the black market: after he learned that 33-year-old Yan Rokotov, the currency king of Moscow, and two young accomplices, had been tried and imprisoned for eight years, he was furious at the leniency of their punishment and, contrary to any concept of justice, he pushed through a review of the case and ultimately secured the death penalty for Rokotov and his gang.

These extreme measures had absolutely no effect on the Soviet public's hankering after contraband goods and hard cash. Rokotov became the hero of various urban legends, including the story that he had been nominated for the Nobel Prize in Economics. New fighters on the frontline of illegal trade appeared in hotels, foreign students' halls of residence and embassies. The black market persisted in the Soviet Union until the collapse of the empire in 1991, when foreign currency became readily available and the country was flooded with imported goods, but the subculture became redundant much earlier. In my view, the raw, 'romantic' black market gradually turned into a business for gangsters and cops. I remember how, in the early 1970s, the 'irons' – as the black market men were called, in Moscow at least – immediately stood out from the general crowd of mods and hippies in the way they wore their clothes. They always looked like models on a catwalk. They were afraid to sit down in case they crumpled their jeans, shirt or jacket – items which, of course, they were only too happy to strip off in the nearest stairwell and sell you at the drop of a hat.

Eventually, together with the more enterprising and career-driven former KGB men and Komsomol leaders, the biggest *fartsovshchiki* became the principal support and power base of a new class of Russian capitalists. Except that, while the KGB and Komsomol men used their party and governmental ties to get rich from supremely lucrative privatisations of factories, land and real estate, the *fartsovshchiki* used their knowledge of foreign languages and experience of actual business to build contacts in finance and trade. I personally know several major Russian bankers who graduated from the black market school. I have no doubt that, had Yan Rokotov been born thirty years later, he would now be the owner of at least one football club and a mega-yacht. A rare occasion when a subcultural background might help you succeed financially!

The Thaw and the Soviet Sixties

To properly understand the *stilyagi* and the black market, however, we need to get some sense of the milieu from which they emerged and of the lives of the majority of young people in this period. For some people the words 'Soviet intelligentsia' are a contradiction in terms. But the Soviet intelligentsia was very much a reality – a thin social layer between the government elite and the working masses. The notion of a 'middle class' did not yet exist in the USSR but this layer had many of its attributes: they were city-dwelling professionals with a higher education, working in science, education and culture. There were subdivisions within this layer: there was an elite of academics, famous musicians and stars of stage and screen; there was a divide between those who worked in the humanities and the engineers and scientists; finally, there was an informal split between the 'genuine' intelligentsia and the 'educationers' *(obrazovanshchina)* – arrivistes from working-class or peasant families who had acquired a university education and intelligentsia professions but not lost their allegedly 'primitive' views and lifestyle.

A Young Tourist badge

Before the war, the remnants of the Russian intelligentsia had lived quietly, without drawing attention to themselves, adapting to the barbaric regime – although this did not save it from the Great Terror of the 1930s. The young generation had barely enough time to stand up on its own two feet before war erupted, slaying millions. The small anti-Stalinist underground had been brutally destroyed. In order for the seeds of revolutionary and democratic thought, scattered by everyone from the *raznochintsy* to the Futurists, to sprout through the cement of Soviet power, what was needed was not just a new generation but a new climate in the country. Everything came together in 1956. In that year, three years after Stalin's death, the famous Thaw began – a short, colourful period of relaxation in government control, presided over by new premier Nikita Khrushchev, which is still the subject of heated debates and bittersweet nostalgia.

The symbols of the era were Sputnik and Yuri Gagarin. Meanwhile, the Thaw's artistic achievements and subcultural drive came from the children of the pre-war baby boom, known thereafter as the *shestidesyatniki*, the 'Sixties Generation'.

The Sixties Generation was a generation of young intellectuals, men and women, from both the humanities and sciences, who emerged at the end of the 1950s, but really only made their mark in the middle of the next decade. They are sometimes called the 'Children of the 20th Congress'. This name refers to the 20th Congress of the Soviet Communist Party, which was held in 1956, and to understand the Sixties Generation you have to understand the importance of this meeting. As we know, it was the Party that drove the totalitarian Soviet Union in every aspect, not only in its ideology, but in economics, science and culture. In theory, the direction of the Party was supposed to be determined by these Congresses, where all the Party members would gather to elect the Central Committee. However, Stalin had felt little need for anything other than his own personal authority and only one Congress was held between 1939 and 1955. The 20th Congress was the first to be held after the tyrant's death, and it was here that Khrushchev gave his famous 'secret speech' in which he spoke out against Stalin's personality cult, his crimes against the people and the gulag. The most high-ranking Communists were probably well aware all along of what had been going on, and many had colluded in these crimes, but the secret speech still had a remarkable effect and the party line changed dramatically. (Similarly, today's Russian elite, and many ordinary Russians too, are fully aware that Putin is a gangster and corrupt liar, but if a high-ranking official spoke out against him at some important forum a new government would, I believe, come to power.)

The people and the intelligentsia reacted to Khrushchev's speech in different ways. There was a wave of suicides around the country, but young people were filled with optimism and inspiration. And history seemed to justify their optimism: 1957 saw the World Festival of Youth and Students, the launch of Sputnik and the beginning of massive construction projects in Siberia. This was accompanied by a loosening of restrictions in culture and art; many great writers and poets emerged; the Cuban Revolution took place right under the noses of the Americans; and Gagarin became the first man in space. Finally, at the 22nd Congress of the Party in 1961, it was solemnly declared that the current generation of Soviet people would live under full Communism! The Thaw felt like a 1950s version of perestroika and it was met with great popular enthusiasm.

You couldn't say that the members of the Sixties Generation were blue-eyed, rosy-cheeked propagandists and builders of Communism. It was more complicated than that. They grew hoarse arguing about Lenin and Stalin, capitalism and socialism and freedom of speech and freedom of creativity – but their attitude was generally positive. In fact this was the last Soviet generation who believed in Communism. Their ideology was

Members of the British delegation to the 6th World Festival of Youth and Students in Moscow, 1957.
Photograph: Valentin Mastyukov, Alexander Konkov / TASS. Courtesy of ITAR-TASS / Archive

almost identical to that of the boys and girls of the underground movement of the 1940s and 1950s who were in favour of Lenin but opposed to Stalin. They stood for democratic, experimental Communism and opposed bureaucracy and dogmatism. Returning to Stoppard's classification of youth movements, they were not exactly heretics – during the Thaw they were pretty much the mainstream – and they weren't quite pagans, but they were certainly romantic. Their cult movie was Marlen Khutsiev's *I Am Twenty*, released in 1965. It drew a direct link between the generation of young people of the early 1920s and those in the early 1960s, who, like them, supported the true ideals of the revolution. As the poet and songwriter Bulat Okudzhava said, "the task of their generation was not to destroy the communist regime but to 'humanise' it".

Bella Akhmadulina at the House of Artists on Kuznetsky Most. Igor Palmin, 1974. Courtesy of the photographer

Pro-Communist but democratic; pro-revolution but categorically against military action; obsessed with the idea of seeing the USSR at the cutting edge, but altogether lacking nationalist feelings – these were the classic views of the Sixties Generation. Some considered this position to be shot through with contradictions, others thought it well-balanced. To me, it always seemed that the Sixties Generation were the direct inheritors of the Futurists: they turned the Futurist poet Mayakovsky into a cult figure, holding poetry readings and demos by his statue; they too were obsessed with the future and experimental in their art and their theatre. Foreign influence wasn't that strong and it came mainly from the leftist, anti-imperialist, anti-war and anti-bourgeois elements of Western culture: Bertolt Brecht, Ernest Hemingway, Louis Aragon and Jean-Paul Sartre, Italian 'Neo-Realism', the 'British Angry Young Men', American protest singers and the 'Beat' poets. Unlike the pagan *stilyagi* who preceded them, and the hippies that followed them – the subject of the next chapter – the Sixties Generation managed to avoid imitation and created a culture that was independent and compelling.

This was possible thanks to the awakening – the thawing perhaps – of some major talents in the country: film directors like Khutsiev and Andrei Tarkovsky, poets like Joseph Brodsky and Bella Akhmadulina, songwriters like Okudzhava and Vladimir Vysotsky. They, and many more besides, were the cultural icons of their age. Poetry readings were held in packed stadiums. Young people waited for every new novel, poem and film like a revelation. Recordings by Okudzhava and Vysotsky were copied from tape recorder to tape recorder thousands of times. What's more, these new icons really were gifted, especially when compared to the boring, institutionalised cultural products of the Stalin period. By not dwelling too much on ideological and historical dogma, the art of the Sixties was, in many ways, reminiscent of the traditions of the Silver Age: they launched into brave experimentation with form, subject and polemical content. Fittingly, many of the major names of the Silver Age, people like Anna Akhmatova and Osip Mandelstam, whose work had long been banned, became relevant again. Artists like Malevich and Kandinsky

Andrei Tarkovsky, 1949

BARDS
(1960s and 1970s)

With their poetic lyrics sung quietly over simple melodies, the songs of these quiet, well-read men were a Thaw-era phenomenon that became a staple of the cultural life of the intelligentsia. The closest Western equivalent would be the folk music of Pete Seeger or Bob Dylan, but the Soviets were even more varied in their lyrics, ranging from the melancholy romances of Bulat Okudzhava to the ironic observations of Yuly Kim, via the political satire of Alexander Galich. The most popular and influential Russian bard was the actor and bon vivant Vladimir Vysotsky, whose songs had everything: horror, sarcasm, love and, above all, an impassioned call for freedom. His funeral in 1980 (he died at only 43) turned into a massive public outpouring of grief and frustration.

The Grushinsky Festival, an annual celebration of the music of 'bards'. Vladimir Kakovkin, 1970s. Courtesy of the Valery Grushin Samara Region Bards Club

The Grushinsky Festival. Vladimir Kakovkin, 1970s.
Courtesy of the Valery Grushin Samara Region Bards Club

saw a resurgence in popularity. The catchphrase in artistic circles was "innovative in form, socialist in content". (One notable exception was Alexander Solzhenitsyn: born in 1918, he was at the older end of the Sixties Generation, and he not only expressed clearly anti-Soviet views but also preferred more traditional forms.)

All this talent was eagerly consumed by an army of simple, intelligent young Soviets, who marched briskly along in the wake of these icons, firmly denying the Stalinist nightmare. They looked towards the future with optimism, something that is generally quite uncharacteristic of Russians. Their energy and desire for change was reminiscent of the *raznochintsy* of the nineteenth century, but their narrow trousers and interest in contemporary Western culture were inherited from the *stilyagi*. They had beards and wore plaid shirts, which they called '*cowboyki*'; they loved hiking and songs round the campfire with guitars; their favourite sport was volleyball and their favourite books were science fiction novels. The space race had given rise to an incredible boom in everything to do with space. A sort of cult grew up around the first cosmonauts and, in among a load of futuristic kitsch, some of the best prose of the period emerged from the pen of two brothers, Arkady and Boris Strugatsky, whose powerful works of science fiction, heavily laden with major ethical questions, remain a favourite source of quotations for the liberal intelligentsia.

Vladimir Vysotsky performing at the Taganka Theatre 15th anniversary concert.
Igor Palmin, April 23, 1979.
Courtesy of the photographer

Unlike other youth subcultures, the Sixties Generation made no delineation between *zapadniki* and Slavophiles. They were almost all 'internationalists', rejecting both Western capitalism and archaic Russia. Although they did have a huge respect, even awe, for Western culture, what was truly sacred to them was their belief in the superiority of the Soviet way of life. Instead, the chief division of the Soviet Sixties remained the aforementioned split between the humanities and the sciences. Public debates, a pastime long forgotten these days, were extremely popular, with themes like: "What is more important – science or art?" In that question, sensational breakthroughs in space exploration, nuclear power and cybernetics gave science the upper hand. Posters of Einstein and Soviet physicist Lev Landau were as popular as those of Gagarin and Fidel Castro. Art, in contrast, had been badly discredited by its toadying up to power in the Stalin era. My parents belonged to this generation and, although they were professional historians, they were insistent that I should study either mathematics or physics at university. They reasoned that I could entertain myself with the study of philosophy or literature in my spare time, like many others, but if I didn't want to be dependent on the government and its ideology and become a 'prostitute' in the humanities, I would need to get a real profession. In the years that followed they were, in many ways, proved right.

The excitement of the Soviet Sixties lasted until 1968, but the atmosphere of undiluted enthusiasm changed to something altogether

Yevgeny Yevtushenko, 1976.
Moscow. USSR.
Poet Yevgeny Yevtushenko
performing. Photograph:
TASS / Valentin Mastyukov;
Vladimir Savostyanov.
Courtesy of ITAR-TASS / Archive

less joyful in the middle of the decade. In September 1964, as a result of a secret palace coup, Khrushchev was packed off into retirement. The younger generation was quite accepting of this – after all, old Nikita was a Stalinist relic, his successors were younger, and the new first deputy premier, Alexei Kosygin, had a sound reputation as an economic reformer. However, it soon became apparent that instead of the colours of socialism being painted in yet brighter tones, they were fading away. The first warning bell came with the very public prosecution of two writers, Yuri Daniel and Andrei Sinyavsky, which ended in February 1966 with the two being sentenced to five years and seven years, respectively, in a labour camp for "anti-Soviet agitation and propaganda". Their only offence was that their pseudonymous satirical prose had been published for several years in the West. The case sparked heated debates in intellectual circles. Sixty-two well-known cultural figures, including many notable representatives of the Soviet Sixties like Bella Akhmadulina and Bulat Okudzhava, published an open letter in defence of the two writers. On 5 December 1965, the day of the celebration of the Soviet Constitution, a small 'Glasnost Meeting' was held on Red Square in support of Sinyavsky and Daniel. The participants were at first detained but quickly released. It seems that those now in power – in what would become known as the Brezhnev regime – were not yet quite sure how best to 'tighten the screws'. But a warning had been sounded.

The shift in mood was evident in the culture of the time. Just two and a half years separate Khutsiev's *I Am Twenty* and his next film, *July Rain* in 1967 (many reviewers rechristened it *I Am Thirty*), but the characters have not only grown up, their passionate arguments, their faith and optimism have been replaced by disappointment, cynicism and alienation. *I Am Twenty* ends with the soldiers of 1917 walking off into a fog – a romantic symbol for the continuation of the revolution. The ending of *July Rain* is a sudden, emotional meeting between war veterans. As I see it, Khutsiev is pointing out how little remains in our lives that is genuine and real. The major literary events of 1966 and 1968 are also indicative of the new paradigm: the first Soviet editions of Kafka and of *The Catcher in the Rye,* and the serialisation of Mikhail Bulgakov's long suppressed *The Master and Margarita*, a dark and mocking dismantling of Soviet reality. The word 'estrangement', which hitherto had meant little to the compassionate intelligentsia, became the order of the day.

The year 1968 seemed to offer a light at the end of the tunnel — the Prague Spring. But, as the joke goes, this light turned out to be the headlights of an oncoming express train. The events in Czechoslovakia, as local leaders attempted to reform Communism from the inside, terrified the Soviet Party elite, seemingly proving to them the deplorable consequences of excessive liberalism. The military invasion of August 1968 put an end to many things, including the Thaw. The Sixties Generation had, on the whole, rapidly welcomed the Czechoslovak slogan of "Socialism with a human face" — this was their dream! — so the clank of the tank tracks on Prague's cobblestones sounded like the tolling of a funeral bell to them. My parents were left disillusioned and I, the young Octobrist, made my first steps in subversion.

In the end, it turned out that the fragile balancing act that was 'humane Communism' lacked any real vitality. It wasn't until the late 1980s that people ever mentioned the Sixties Generation again: some of them experienced a real renaissance during Gorbachev's glasnost — they made public speeches, published books and some even became politicians — finally taking their revenge on the Soviet system for the defeats of the 1960s (alas, yet again, only a temporary one!). This was their swan song, but I am glad that it was sung.

Most of the ordinary rank-and-file of the Sixties Generation, the bright-eyed hikers and sci-fi fans, smoothly transitioned into the dejected, cynical and inebriated category of people known as the 'Soviet intelligentsia of the era of stagnation'. They were a world away from the new generation of hippies and rockers that shared the streets with them. The cultural figureheads of the era split into two camps. Half went into emigration or exile, like Alexander Solzhenitsyn and Andrei Tarkovsky, while others — Bulat Okudzhava, Marlen Khutsiev, the Strugatskys — stayed, but fell into semi-oblivion, their voices muted. Only a tiny part of the 'army of the Thaw' continued to fight for freedom, human rights and 'a human face' on power. This was the intelligentsia in the classical, nineteenth-century meaning of the word — a conscientious, idealistic and selfless section of society. Like the Populists before them, they had little or no political or economic agenda. Like the Decembrists, they had little in common with the ordinary people. I don't know who it was who first gave them their name — most likely it was some Western journalist — but they began to be known as 'dissidents'.

David Bowie in Moscow. Geoff MacCormack, 1973. Courtesy of the photographer

"We were given a list of dos and don'ts
when we arrived in Siberia to board the
Trans-Siberian Express, what we could
and couldn't photograph, so David
was breaking a whole stack of rules
by filming the event, considering the
amount of military hardware on show.
That's why he's looking a little furtive."

Geoff MacCormack

CHAPTER 7

Heretics and Pagans II: Dissidents and Music across the Iron Curtain. 1960–1980

I hesitated for a long time before deciding to write about the dissidents as a subculture. They are of course a very well-known Russian phenomenon, and much has been written about their movement and about their unwavering insistence on being different and getting angry. But they were far from young and there wasn't much that made them stand out: the dissidents had no dress code. I doubt that anyone could picture the dance floor at a dissident party. The only music that I associate with them is the sung poetry of so-called bards like Alexander Galich. To read: a little bit of political poetry and fiction, as well as human rights materials and anti-Stalinist samizdat (illegal self-published literature – perhaps the sole material symbol of the dissident movement).

The dissidents were a solely political and ethical offshoot of the Sixties Generation. There were far fewer of them, of course. It's difficult to say exactly how many there were. If you type the question "How many dissidents were there in the USSR?" into a search engine, the internet comes up with: "In the period from 1956 to 1987, 8,145 people were convicted under the criminal code relating to anti-Soviet activity." But I think that far from all of these were real dissidents, and not every real dissident was ever convicted. In other words, there were not many of them, perhaps just a few thousand. Men and women were equally well represented – perhaps for the only time in the history of Russian politics – but only about 20% of them, and none of the leaders, were from the younger generation. Why? I would like to propose two rather bold theses here. First, in the years when dissident activity was at its height, the younger generation had more interesting things to think about than politics – as we'll see later in the chapter. Second, the dissident movement itself had something of a 'mature' air about it; it was almost too grown up and stuffy. Having said that, it all started energetically enough. The origin of Soviet dissidence could be said to be the 'Mayak movement'. In 1958, a statue of the Futurist poet Mayakovsky was erected in one of Moscow's central squares. He was one of the Sixties Generation's most important heroes, and soon the 'mayaki' began gathering at the foot of the statue for spontaneous

The Russian dissident, Vladimir Bukovsky arriving at London Airport on his way to stay with actor David Markham, one of the principal campaigners for his release, 4th January 1976. Photo by Central Press/ Getty Images

discussions which, more often than not, ended with heated political debates about Stalin, the Revolution, the role of youth and the inflexibility of the Komsomol. It was here in 1960 that 18-year-old Vladimir Bukovsky, future enfant terrible of Soviet dissidence and a fiery orator, made his first appearances. While most of the people holding these discussions were young people with 'progressive' Communist convictions, there were also Trotskyites, anarchists and pro-Western liberals – it was Soviet Moscow's take on Hyde Park's Speaker's Corner. The Mayakovsky monument was kept under constant observation by intelligence officers and the *mayaki* were regularly dispersed by the police and the KGB. However, in 1965 Bukovsky and the young poets of the neo-Futurist group 'SMOG' (the initials are said to represent the Russian words 'Courage, Thought, Image, and Depth') began giving public readings and holding meetings here in defence of unofficial art. It was the people at these readings, shored up by a large group of students from Moscow State University who made up the majority of the participants at the Glasnost Meeting in 1965.

Soon afterwards, Bukovsky and other young protesters were arrested for the first time. The authorities turned to the now infamous resort of 'punitive psychiatry' and had Bukovsky declared insane. He was incarcerated for eight months in a psychiatric hospital. For the authorities this was a smart move, of course. Instead of a heroic uprising of dissidents, the meeting was made out to be just a bunch of crazies. Also, it was subconsciously being made known that to hate the Soviet system, and to fight it, was plain insanity. The last notable public demonstration was on 25 August 1968, in protest at the crushing of the Prague spring and in support of "your freedom and ours", as the slogan went. Only eight people went out onto the square with banners: they were all arrested, beaten and imprisoned – two in a mental hospital and five more in labour camps or exile. Only one was released, the 21-year-old girlfriend of one of the protesters. It was after this historic moment that the dissident movement took on its most recognisable form. Strange as it may seem, the underlying principle of practically all dissident activity was to obey Soviet laws. The basic idea was that the Soviet Constitution and its code of laws were perfectly just; the problem was that the authorities were not adhering to them. Hence the decision to hold the Glasnost Meeting on the official Day of the Constitution. The Soviet dissidents were motivated by a desire for strict compliance with the law, using non-violence, openness, letters and petitions. Possibly the only thing they did that contravened these principles was their samizdat publications. The dissidents were not just heretics, they were very disciplined heretics. For this they have been much criticised. Moldovan dissident, Vasile Ernu, described dissidence as "the product of a collaboration between Soviet form and anti-Soviet content". Cultural historians Pyotr Vail and Alexander Genis have examined all the dissidents' texts, and came to the paradoxical conclusion that their "declaration of protest was pretty much copied word for word from Party

Opening of the Mayakovsky monument, 19.07.1958. Courtesy of the Archive of Memorial International

documents – just going in the opposite direction". This is exactly why they were, as I said, stuffy, boring and unattractive. I have found myself in the company of dissidents a few times in the past and always felt nothing in common with them: they were generally glum and spoke grimly. Their agenda – rejecting Soviet power and helping friends who were in prison or disgraced – was important to me. But the way it was all being carried out reminded me of some sort of doomed sect. I remember being surprised that they had nothing very interesting to say about the situation in the country, not to mention abroad. Every conversation centred on particular people, their behaviour and relationships. Perhaps the matriarch of the human rights movement Lyudmila Alexeyeva was right when she said that the dissident movement was moral rather than political in nature. It was nevertheless very diverse: it was sort of a Noah's Ark on which anyone could be rescued from the Soviet deluge, regardless of ideology. Everyone was against the regime, but what they stood for varied from person to person, ranging from anarchism to monarchism. Alexeyeva proposed a popular classification of the political spectrum of dissidents:

- Liberal democrats – supporters of the Western path to development.
- Left-wing reforming communists – also called the "Euro communists" or "the new left".
- National minorities (from the Baltic states, Ukraine, Georgia and so on) – campaigning for freedom from imperial domination.
- Russian nationalists – monarchists and campaigners against Communist internationalism.
- Religious dissidents – Orthodox believers, Baptists and ecumenists.
- Zionists and Jewish refuseniks.

Then came what was probably the majority: people with vague but convinced anti-Soviet views. I had close friends among those on the 'left' and among the 'Orthodox believers'. The left-wing dissidents were about my age, around twenty, and members of a group known as the 'Young Socialists'. Devotees of Che Guevara and revolutionary existentialism, they would come to our house to visit my father, a Marxist theorist who was something of a guru for them. At the beginning of the 1980s the KGB came after them: I remember that one lad, Oleg, one of the most enthusiastic, was killed in suspicious circumstances. The others were arrested and questioned. And it is at moments like this that we see signs of the moral degradation of Russian revolutionary youth over the preceding one hundred years: unlike the doughty fighters for the cause in the nineteenth century, many of my contemporaries immediately started to waver, repent and turn informant. Informing on, among others, my father. The same thing happened with the religious dissidents. It was the very person who introduced me to the congregation around the 'alternative' priests Alexander Men and Dmitry Dudko that then went on and denounced me for being involved with them. The practices of informing on others and spreading disinformation were a huge part of dissident life. One friend of mine, who was caught in possession of samizdat material, was told he would be expelled from his institute unless he became an informer. He rather proudly told me that he regularly named names – but only of people he believed were informers themselves. So what exactly did the dissidents do? They fought back against the KGB and helped comrades who were in need; they had connections with the Western media and human rights organisations; they printed and distributed human rights literature (to a very small audience). Strictly speaking, that's about all they did – and one cannot but feel that there is a gaping hole here. Soviet dissidents, from 1968 right up to the collapse of the movement in the mid-1980s, never got involved in stirring up public protest or spreading the word. They never tried to expand their ranks and made no attempt, not even a symbolic one, to 'go to the people', as the Populists had done, generally preferring to exist in splendid isolation. What is strange about this is that, from the 1970s onwards, gentle disenchantment with the Soviet project became a way of life for pretty much everyone, not just the younger generation and urban intellectuals. People respected dissidents. They heard all about them from melodramatic radio programmes on Voice of America or the BBC and thought of them as legendary figures. But the dissidents failed to meet the people halfway, perhaps because they didn't really know or understand the people at all. You can argue forever about the significance and legacy of the dissident movement. I don't agree with the cynical idea that dissidents were just a handful of half-crazy bores who lived off Western funds and whose only role in the USSR was to annoy the KGB. No, they were noble, self-sacrificing and selfless and suffered greatly for their beliefs. A suffering which often cost them their health and sometimes their lives. In my view, they undoubtedly played a part in giving focus to resistance against the regime, although this role was more symbolic than practical. But I think that the dissidents' commitment to adhering to the letter of the law, to fighting the enemy by the enemy's own rules, was a compromise and a mistake. Unfortunately, this flawed idea became very widespread and damaged the DNA of the Russian protest movement for decades to come. The complete failure of the anti-Putin opposition movement in 2011 and 2012 can largely be explained by the fact that it faithfully followed the old dissident precepts.

A passport belonging to 16-year-old Almaty resident Ablikim Akmullaev, who has signed himself "Pink Floyd", 1981.
Now an artist, Akmullaev describes how a year of listening to Pink Floyd's 1980 album *The Wall* led him to identify with the album's protagonist, Pink. "I had fully entered into Pink's existence, so it was quite natural for me to sign myself 'Pink Floyd'. My school teacher told me I'd ruined my life." He spent most of the 1980s under the spell of Pink Floyd, even ending up in court as a result of his "psychedelic experiments". "For those nine years I lived life to the full. And I've got no regrets. On the contrary, I'm grateful to the Floyd for everything I learned."

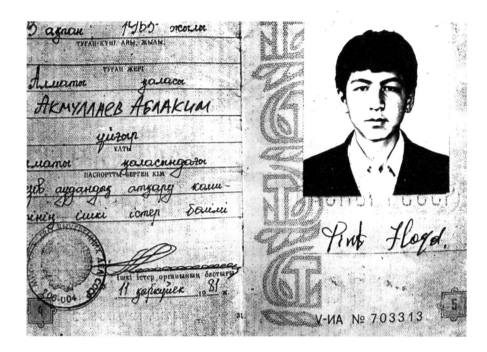

Music from across the Iron Curtain

At the same time as a small number of dissidents were pursuing a strategy of heretical resistance to Soviet power, a genuinely popular movement was undermining young people's commitment to the Soviet cause. And it was all down to music.

It was music which, in the 1960s, ushered in a new, global phase in the subcultural history of Russia. While other subcultures we have seen – dandyism, for instance – have had a European scale, they have always had a specifically Russian identity. In what other country could you have found the Populists, the Bolsheviks or the science-loving Sixties Generation? Even the *stilyagi* were the children of Iron Curtain isolation. Despite imitating the West in some ways, members of these subcultures had differed fundamentally from their peers in the rest of the world. During the Khrushchev Thaw, Russia, now a superpower, became a part of the global community, whether it wanted to or not (albeit in a rather problematic and muted way). And the main point of entry the world had into this once inaccessible country was music. In the second half of the twentieth century music became as motivating and, surprisingly, as intellectual a force among young people as literature and poetry had been in the previous century – and perhaps the internet is now. This was thanks to a happy combination of events such as the development of the recording industry, the invention of electronic musical instruments, the fall of racial barriers in music, the talent and courage of young artists and a growing sense of identity among young people. This final factor was directly related to an economic breakthrough: for the first time in the history of our civilisation, a teenage marketplace appeared and started making itself known in no uncertain terms.

Young people, first in the affluent United States and then in Europe, felt that they were financially independent enough to decide for themselves what they wanted to buy, to wear and to listen to. And so the battle between 'the young' and 'the grownups' was fought out on the battlefield of music and clothes. On the one hand, there was rock and roll and jeans and on the other, Sinatra and suits. The Soviet Union has always been particularly proud of being a monolithic society, with no clash of the generations, but in the mid-1960s a clear gap formed between old and young.

The chief vehicle for the cultural globalisation of the Soviet Union and the catalyst for the new generation gap was The Beatles. They played as important a role in the life of Soviet youth as Lord Byron had in the lives of the creative, romantic Russian nobles of the early nineteenth century. Why The Beatles? I will quote here from my own book *Back in the USSR: The True Story of Rock in Russia*:

"The Beatles had melodies, and for the Russian ear that is mandatory. The Beatles' happy, harmonious vocal choir proved to be just the voice for which our confused generation was waiting, but was unable to create for itself. Liverpool delivered the solution. The well-known phrase "They must be Russians'" would have suited The Beatles splendidly – as is indicated by the phenomenal response to their music by our entire youth audience. I've often heard one and the same phrase from many different people: The Beatles hit the bullseye. Yes, they had everything, and if you want to feel what millions of lonely Russian hearts were lacking so terribly, just listen to *She Loves You*. Joy, rhythm, beauty, spontaneity. In a word, 'love'."

Fans of The Beatles were known as *'bitlomany'* – Beatlemaniacs. At first they resembled an updated version of the *stilyagi*, with long hair instead of quiffs, and Nehru jackets instead of check sports jackets. But it soon became clear that there were two important differences in quality and quantity. There were far more Beatles fans than there had been *stilyagi* – in fact there were hundreds and thousands of them, if not millions. And it wasn't enough for them to just listen and dance to their favourite music – they wanted to play and to sing as well. The Beat invasion in the USSR happened on a massive scale, but took the form of a sort of underground partisan movement. Previously, there had been absolutely no fashionable Anglo-American music in the Soviet Union – no Beatles, no Rolling Stones, no Beach Boys, nothing. At least not from official sources like radio, TV and magazines. You could only listen to your idols from the West on shortwave radio stations like Voice of America, get their records from the black market where they cost a fortune, or buy them on cassette. Cassette players appeared in shops in the early 1960s and, along with The Beatles, became the most important element of the musical revolution in the Soviet Union.

Soviet records of The Beatles and Foreign Pop, Melodia Records

Members of the intelligentsia listened to vaguely anti-Soviet songs by bards like Vladimir Vysotsky; youngsters listened to rock music, which back then we called "big beat". If the powers that be and the KGB had known what all this would lead to, they would probably have banned the manufacture of tape recorders. But by then it was too late.

The Beatlemaniac vanguard was actually made up of musicians, who had to make their own electric guitars by sawing up bits of wood and vandalising cinema sound systems to get the necessary parts. Thousands of pianos were taken apart to plunder the strings for bass guitars. It's hard to believe, but, by 1969, Moscow's Beat Club had 263 bands on its register – an explosion of interest in music matched in other cities in the Soviet Union. These Beat groups were mostly formed by students and they performed at dances and parties. The authorities couldn't keep track of them and they didn't leave any recordings behind, which is no real loss as they only sang cover versions. In a sense, in the absence of imported records and discos (Moscow's first disco night – which I ran – started in 1972) they played the role of live juke boxes for music-starved youngsters. If we disregard the impressive scale of this, then it all resembled a direct continuation of the *stilyagi* story: music, dancing, having fun, getting a buzz – the form as thrilling as possible but with zero content. Believe me, the majority of the Russian Beat groups of that time barely understood what they were singing about. They didn't speak English and learned songs purely phonetically. I even helped out a few Moscow bands by writing out English-language song lyrics for them in Cyrillic. After nearly ten years, something resembling content began to appear – the Russian Beat scene survived *stilyagi* syndrome – and it turned out to be even more exotic than the form.

The 1970s is often considered a period of 'stagnation' in Soviet history: there was an ageing Politburo, headed by the boring Brezhnev; there were no great achievements but no great failures either; in a time of enormous shortages, the population spent their time slogging around the shops looking for food and other vital products. But young people were buzzing with excitement, completely cut off from the concerns of the adults. Two interrelated factors dominated their lives: the phenomenal popularity of Western music, which included rock, disco and all sorts of exotic Italian pop and a new alternative ideology – hippiedom.

The authorities, in this case the Komsomol and the Ministry of Culture, tried with all their might to prevent the wave of Western music from taking hold. They encouraged 'ideologically correct' surrogate rock-groups – the so-called vocal instrumental ensembles (VIEs) who sang optimistic Soviet songs but with a modern "electric" arrangement. The giant Soviet record monopoly Melodia bought the licence to sell innocuous Western records by the likes of ABBA; acts such as Cliff Richard, Elton John and Boney M were allowed over on tour. In short, they were clearly laying their bets on the light entertainment of 'positive' pop and disco, right at the peak of popularity of 'destructive' rock. Discos sprung up everywhere and the so-called 'discotheque movement' became an obsession in the USSR. Thousands of discos appeared in state run Houses of Culture, student clubs and even in factories and village halls.

The Komsomol quickly took control of them, censoring the music and doing everything it could to include this 'new form of youth leisure activity' in its ideological work. A typical Soviet disco went something like this: first the DJ would give a propagandist speech denouncing the dangers and failings of imperialism in all its forms – American aggression, unemployment in Britain, strikes in France – all the while showing slides of bombings and homeless people. This speech would be accompanied by the music from the DJ's favourite band, which was usually Pink Floyd or some other prog-rock. After an hour of this, the long-awaited dance would finally begin, but even this was not so simple: the playlist was required to meet a quota whereby the lion's share of the music was Soviet or from "fraternal socialist countries" and only 5–10% of the repertoire could be from Western groups. I attended dozens of these depressing evenings while researching my PHD on – I know this sounds ridiculous – 'the social efficacy of the discotheque'.

Strangely enough, hippies appeared in the USSR as a result of state propaganda. American hippies were a great ideological gift to the Soviet media. On the one hand, they protested against the Vietnam war, burnt their army draft cards and were opposed to the capitalist establishment. Good for them. On the other hand, they looked awful (according to our commentators), used drugs and indulged in debauchery – all of which perfectly illustrated the decaying of Western society. So towards the end of the 1960s a whole range of these 'sweet and sour' reports on these scary Western rebels appeared, describing how they had hair down to their waists and long beards, wore anti-war symbols pinned to their chests and always had a joint on the go. The propagandists were pretty happy with themselves, but they had failed to anticipate one very important point: Soviet youngsters found this hippie image irresistibly attractive and they immediately became role models for a generation of Soviet wannabes. Hippiedom was incredibly popular in the USSR throughout the first half of the 1970s, and only began to lose impetus towards the beginning of the 1980s. In the West hippies are often talked about as a movement, but our hippies didn't move anywhere in particular because they didn't have any goals in life – it was a purely apolitical subculture. Despite some obvious differences, they had a lot in common with the *stilyagi*, so it is hardly surprising that Alexei Kozlov, one of the greatest *stilyagi*, was just as enthusiastic about the hippie vibe. The main thing the *stilyagi* and the hippies had in common was that they both wanted to provoke the philistine proles around them and to stand out from the crowd. The easiest way to do this was with what they wore and what they listened to – dancing was a thing of the past.

А ТЕПЕРЬ О «ЖУКАХ»

Кто же они, эти загадочные «жуки», имеющие такую фантастическую популярность? — спросил читатель. Увы, это всего-навсего английский эстрадный ансамбль «Битлз» (жуки), состоящий из четырех человек — Джорджа Харрисона, Поля Маккартни, Джона Леннена и Ринго Стара. Трое с гитарами, один ударник — и все четверо... чуть было не сказал — поют! Трудно себе даже представить, какие звуки издают эти молодые люди под собственный аккомпанемент, какое содержание в этих опусах. Достаточно сказать, что одна из их песенок называется «Катись, Бетховен!».

Когда «битлз» испускают свои твистовые крики, молодежь начинает визжать от восторга, топать ногами и свистеть. Тысячи американских подростков так подвывают своим любимцам, что тех еле слышно, несмотря на усилители. Поклонницы, сидя в партере, так сильно дергаются в ритме твиста, что часто впадают в обморочное состояние и просто валятся с кресел.

Обслуживают «жуков» 12 служащих — «пчел», пятеро из них ведут корреспонденцию. Есть пчела-фотограф, есть редактор, выпускающий ежемесячный журнал «Битлз»...

Бедные наивные «жуки»! Вы, на-верно, твердо уверены в том, что все это — слава, бешеные деньги, рев и визг поклонников, визиты к королям — все это навсегда и по заслугам. Но готов биться об заклад, что протянете вы еще год-полтора, а потом появятся молодые люди с еще более дурацкими прическами и дикими голосами, и все кончится!..

И придется вам с трудом пристраиваться в маленькие провинциальные кабачки на временную работу или идти «пчелами» к новым «жукам»...

А вот что касается Бетховена, то-го самого, которого вы в вашей песенке так настойчиво призывали «катиться», то за него, я думаю, можно быть спокойным.

P. S. Если вы заметили, дорогой читатель, у меня в заголовке к слову «жуки» произвольно добавлен эпитет — навозные, но мне почему-то кажется, что вы не осудите меня за эту вольность. Тем более, что по этому поводу мы вам кое-что объяснили.

Никита БОГОСЛОВСКИЙ

«Жуки» прибыли в Соединенные Штаты. Карикатура из газеты «Нью-Йорк геральд трибюн».

And now about The Beatles,
Literaturnaya Gazeta,
December 1964

Who are they, these mysterious 'beetles', who are so fantastically popular? – the reader might ask. Alas, it's only the English pop group The Beatles, which consists of four people – George Harrison, Paul McCartney, John Lennon, and Ringo Starr. Three of them play guitar, one plays the drums – and all four…. I almost said 'sing'! It is hard even to imagine the sounds emitted by these young men to their own accompaniment, or what these opuses actually mean. Suffice it to say that one of their songs is called "Scram, Beethoven!"

When the 'beetles' emit their twisted cries, the youth begins to squeal with delight and stomp and whistle. Thousands of American teenagers howl at their heroes so loudly that their own sounds are barely audible, despite the amplifiers. Groupies sitting in the stalls twitch to the rhythm of the twist so much that they often pass out or simply fall out of their chairs.

The 'beetles' are served by twelve employees – 'bees'. Five of them deal with correspondence. There is also a bee-photographer and an editor who publishes a monthly magazine, The Beatles…

Poor, naïve 'beetles'! You must truly believe that all of this – fame, fortune, roaring and screeching fans, visits to kings – is not only deserved but will last forever. But I'm ready to bet that in a year, or year and a half, there will be young people with even wackier hairstyles and wild voices, and it'll all be over for you!

And you'll have to work hard to get temporary work in local pubs or become 'bees' to the new 'beetles'.

And as for Beethoven, the very man who you tell so insistently to 'scram' in your song, I think we can stop worrying about him.

P.S. You may have noticed, dear reader, that I have arbitrarily added the epithet 'dung' to the word 'beetles' in the headline, but somehow I think you will not blame me for taking this liberty. Moreover, on this occasion, we have given you an explanation.

Nikita Bogoslovsky

Hippies on Palace Square, Leningrad. From the "peoplebook" of Sasha the Artist. Aleksandr Iosifov, 1978. Courtesy of the artist

The music they liked was exclusively Western (north American and British) and their clothes were imported. There was one more thing they had in common: the Soviet hippies' ideology, as with the early-period *stilyagi*, didn't include any deeply held humanitarian beliefs, but was focused on an obsession with cool music and cool clothes. Our hippies had no idea about people like Timothy Leary, Ken Kesey or Herbert Marcuse. Perhaps the Russian hippies' only guru was American pop mystic Carlos Castaneda – but his books only began to penetrate the Iron Curtain in the 1980s. The whole ideological foundation of our hippies could be reduced to a few simple, but powerful tenets: stand up against war, make love freely and plentifully, go crazy about music and dress in a way that shocks ordinary Soviet citizens. We hear a lot about hippies and drugs, but they were not used widely in the USSR and the most notorious drug of all, LSD, was impossible to get hold of. Hippie slang was also reminiscent of *stilyagi* jargon but was more extensive because of the number of Russianised English words, like *men* (man), *gerla* (girl) and *flet* (flat). The word *'fak'* became incredibly popular. The hippies had all sorts of places to hang out: they would gather in squares and parks in the centre of town and would sit there all day, smoking, swapping clothes and mingling together peacefully.

The advent of the hippie brought something new and unprecedented to the history of Russian subcultures. For a start, the scale of the movement was huge. The hippies of the 1970s were the largest 'international' subculture our country has ever seen. When Yuri Shevchuk from the group DDT sang "we have hippies in our village" he was not exaggerating. Of course, there was a hippie elite too – the so-called 'centrals' or 'the system'. There were even informal leaders, like Yura Solntse in Moscow and Gena Zaitsev in Leningrad, and popular hippie musicians – but this was just the tip of the iceberg. The hippie style – hair, music, flares, slang – was everywhere. And just as it had been impossible to put a stop to the *stilyagi*, so nothing could be done with the hippies – although there were some half-hearted attempts, such as arrests for antisocial behaviour and enforced haircuts, mostly in the provinces. Later on the hippies started moving around a lot, especially in the summer and normally by hitchhiking. They went travelling together in large groups in two directions: west, to the more Westernised Baltic republics (the Estonian capital Tallinn had a green hill in the heart of the city, known simply as 'The Hill', which became a cult gathering place for hippies from all over the country), and south to the Crimea, because it was warm.

Another difference between hippies and *stilyagi* was that the hippies were more creative, although they didn't actually produce anything very memorable. Thousands of hippie bands played Jimi Hendrix, Santana, Deep Purple and so on. There were a lot of hippie artists too, mostly surrealist, and some of them exhibited in the famous open-air exhibition in Izmailovo Park in 1974, which became known as the 'Bulldozer Exhibition' after the authorities' chosen means of shutting it down. But the most popular artistic enterprise was applied art: a lot of hippies earned their living by designing their own fashionable, scandalous clothes and making their own jewellery. They made them for friends and for sale at markets. Incidentally, the gender balance among the hippies was perfect. In fact, I can't think of any other subculture in Russia, let alone a music-based one, where there were the same number of young men and women.

Their attitude to the Soviet Union and its culture was either one of indifference or was contemptuously negative. There were some exceptions to this rule, but very few – they liked the films of Tarkovsky, the writings of Vasily Aksyonov and the Strugatsky brothers and the productions of the Taganka Theatre. Everything else that was of Soviet origin, from shoes to art, was simply ignored. This was internal emigration in its purest form and it often culminated in actual emigration abroad. I remember how, from the mid-1970s on, many of my friends and acquaintances, including some famous underground musicians, started quietly leaving the country – some of them by marrying foreign citizens and others on Israeli visas. However, all of the above refers to die-hard hippies; there were also millions of hippie hangers-on who weren't too worried about Soviet power and were happy enough to listen to the 'official' surrogate rock culture, whether it was the jolly vocal instrumental ensembles or the Beat-style cartoon film *The Musicians of Bremen*, and to wear Soviet-made platforms (although they would of course have really preferred ones like David Bowie's).

What influence did the hippies have on Russian life and what contribution did they make to Russian culture? Unlike either the Soviet dissidents or the American hippies, Russian hippies made absolutely no mark on politics. Their protests were unformed, unorganised and

confusing for the authorities; all they did was irritate. The only worthwhile cultural product created by the hippies of the 1970s that I can think of is a wonderful play by Boris Grebenshchikov called *Embraced by Jeans*, which was written in 1972 and which poked fun at the life of Soviet hippies in all its diversity, including the informers and the black marketeers. Grebenshchikov (or 'BG' as he is known in Russia) was an important part of Russian hippiedom: an amazing rock lyricist and, for forty years, frontman of legendary Russian band *Aquarium*, he was one of the few pillars of strength of that hippie culture.

But so what? In my opinion the most important and truly amazing thing about Soviet hippiedom, the thing that made it a truly pagan phenomenon, is that it was so widespread: at one point somewhere between 1972 and 1975 it was pretty much a normal way of life for many different young people. This was the first and last time this ever happened under the Soviet regime, and the fact that it was possible at all says a lot about the extreme precariousness of the moral foundations of late Soviet society. And about why these foundations could crumble so quickly.

Boris Grebenshchikov of the band Aquarium, Leningrad. Igor Mukhin. 1986. Courtesy of the author

Izmailovo exhibition. Vladimir Sichov, 1974. Courtesy of the photographer

The first Rock March Across Lithuania, Dinamo stadion, Vilnius. Raimondas Urbakavičius, July 6, 1987. Courtesy of the author

CHAPTER 8

Ten Years That Shook the World: Perestroika and Russian Rock. 1981–1991

There are lots of theories explaining the origins of perestroika, the reforms in the running of the USSR in the mid-1980s which precipitated the collapse of the empire. Many are congratulated for it and many are blamed. Some point to Ronald Reagan, for derailing the Soviet economy with the arms race. Others claim it was the work of Mikhail Gorbachev, who was either a clever strategist or a Western spy, depending who you talk to. Other theories cite factors like the war in Afghanistan, oil prices or the work of the dissidents and nefarious intelligence agencies. Personally my favourite argument – and I'm not saying it's necessarily accurate – is that it was rock and roll that brought freedom to the USSR. (If you don't believe me, you should check out Leslie Woodhead's film *How The Beatles Rocked The Kremlin.*) The theory goes like this: it was rock music that shaped the self-awareness and the tastes of young people in the Soviet Union from the 1960s on, turning it away from totalitarian discipline and towards freedom, replacing the dogmas of the Komsomol with peace and love and substituting Soviet greyness for the technicolour vibrancy of the West. In this sense, both Beatlemania and the hippie movement did their bit in undermining the USSR – at the very least a lot more than the CIA ever did. But music's decisive contribution to changing the country came in the 1980s, from the homegrown bands that made up the movement known simply as Russian Rock.

The first rock bands to sing meaningful songs in Russian only appeared in the early 1970s. The most important of them was Time Machine. They made their debut in 1969, when they were still school kids, but within a few years they were at the forefront of Moscow's underground rock scene. The group's frontman, architecture student Andrei Makarevich, laid the foundation of the Russian Rock style. The formula was simple but very effective: take the music of traditional Anglo-American rock, anything from The Beatles to Led Zeppelin, and mix it with a lyrical sensibility taken from Russian literature and the sung poetry of the bards. Makarevich, like most of Russian rock pioneers, came from a typical Soviet Sixties intelligentsia family; until his father brought the

PERESTROIKA

By the mid-1980s, as has often happened in Russian history, inept management, economic problems and senseless wars (this time in Afghanistan) had put the country in a desperate position. The situation demanded swift and radical changes and Mikhail Gorbachev, the new, relatively young leader of the Soviet government, began to introduce reforms in 1985. At first it looked like a repeat of the Thaw – 'socialism with a human face', the freeing up of culture, flirting with the West – but this time the process went a lot further: Gorby's proclaimed principle of 'openness' meant actual freedom of speech, private enterprise was permitted and the Berlin Wall came down. Just as importantly, the Communist Party lost its monopoly on ideology, which precipitated its rapid decline. By 1990 the Kremlin had lost control of the situation, especially with independence movements growing in strength in the Baltic republics and the Caucasus. The ultimate result was the collapse of the USSR and, logically enough, the end of perestroika itself.

Mike Naumenko, 1987.
Courtesy of the author

album *A Hard Day's Night* back as a gift from a trip abroad, he liked to listen to the satirical, philosophical ballads of Alexander Galich and Bulat Okudzhava. It's no surprise, then, that Time Machine's breakout single, "Fighting with Fools", written when Makarevich was 19, wasn't about girls, dancing or motorbikes, but was a lament for the few remaining smart and honest people on the planet. Their first true hit, however, was their next song, "Puppets" (1974), a barefaced satire about dull, obedient and silent citizens whose strings are pulled from above. (It's a song that people still sing today – it's just as relevant as ever.) Nevertheless, despite Time Machine's good example and the existence of a few other black sheep, like the Leningrad groups Myths and Saint Petersburg, the music scene continued to be dominated by copycat bands singing in bad English.

It was in 1979 that Russian Rock finally emerged from the underground. First, Time Machine and a few other Russian-language rock groups were given professional status and could now officially perform in big concert venues. Second, a whole new musical culture sprang up in Leningrad which started producing songs with Russian lyrics and a contemporary sound modelled on punk and new wave. The Baltic city became the undisputed capital of Russian Rock and was home to an explosion in '*magnitizdat*' – the illicit copying of songs from cassette to cassette, the parallel record industry which back in the 1960s had helped The Beatles and Vysotsky find new fans. But bands also started making real albums in proper recording studios, with cover art and track lists: these were real LPs, not released on vinyl but on tapes and cassettes, with photographs of the musicians and their friends glued on the front. This was a huge step forward when compared to dissident samizdat publishing – not only in packaging but in the scale and in the speed of production. The most popular albums were copied in their hundreds and thousands and dispatched from Leningrad to Vladivostok in a day. Unlike altruistic samizdat, *magnitizdat* usually had a commercial basis: professional sound engineers had a dozen or so tape recorders whirring away around the clock in their homes. Andrei Tropillo, a sound engineer who worked in the local headquarters of the Pioneers, the Soviet scout equivalent, led the way in the illegal LP trade: while he was on the night shift, rock musicians would come and visit his studio. Many of the singers and bands on that night shift went on to become legends like Aquarium, Kino and Mike Naumenko. Their music was very different from Makarevich's innocent, melodious, poetic songs. Their lyrics were closer to Lou Reed and Bob Dylan – cynical and down-to-earth:

> I'm sitting in the outhouse, reading Rolling Stone,
> Venechka's in the kitchen pouring samogon,
> Vera's asleep upstairs but the tape recorder's blaring,
> It's time someone woke her up, but that would be *mauvais ton*,
> Another day of rain, I want to sleep, but I'm past caring,
> I want to smoke, but all my cigs are gone.

That is how Mike Naumenko's song "Suburban Blues" begins. Young Russians had started singing about alcohol and drugs. And sex, too, though not in this song. The new Leningrad rock was a sensation in the early Eighties and soon became notorious. This popularity inspired some strange developments, not least the fact that the newly opened Leningrad Rock Club in 1981 – a place that would become a mecca for young Russians – was supported by the KGB. The authorities clearly thought that this would make it easier to control this crazy young mob. But all the mob cared about was that there was finally somewhere where they could see all their favourite groups perform on a regular basis – the only place like it in the whole Soviet Union.

In 1981 the two-year 'mini-Thaw' which had accompanied the Moscow Olympics of 1980 came to an end, ushering in a depressing new era. This was the time of the Soviet war in Afghanistan, the confrontation with Reagan, the economic crash and empty shelves in the shops. The government tightened the screws wherever possible. One of the principal targets of this crackdown was rock and roll: the authorities were clearly alarmed by its massive popularity and the totally uncontrollable underground recording industry, not to mention the outrageous lyrics. The government's assault on rock took a classical form: extensive blacklists of musicians were drawn up; unofficial concerts were raided and arrests made; some rock musicians (and even more promoters) were locked up behind bars; the mass media was forbidden to even print the word 'rock'. But the authorities were powerless in the face of the creative drive of the rockers and the enthusiasm of their fans. Despite the efforts of informers, secret concerts, *kvartirniki* were regularly held in private apartments and out-of-town dachas.

Those few years from 1980 to 1984 were as significant for Russian Rock as 1965 to 1969 was in the West. In other words, it was in that period that most of the genre's classic hits were written, at a time when many musicians had no electric guitars to plug in and drummers rapped out the beat on their knees. It is quite telling that Russian Rock's creative peak came during this period of adversity. The icons of the time were the brooding Viktor Tsoi from Kino, the brilliant poet Alexander Bashlachev, the psychedelic holy fool Pyotr Mamonov, the provincial preacher Yuri Shevchuk, and Zhanna Aguzarova, a sort of martian *stilyaga* whose outrageous stylings anticipated Lady Gaga by about thirty years. They all made their first appearances in the desperate years of the early Eighties and wrote many of their best songs.

There were two factors at work here. First, ambitious young people had only one option – to go underground. This was the only excitement available in the USSR at the time! Everything else was in decline – colourless and catastrophically boring. Who cares about money or a career when there's nothing to buy and all the best jobs are taken by the stick-in-the-mud older generation? There was sex and vodka, of course, but for some people this wasn't enough – they wanted action, they wanted to do something meaningful with their lives. Second, if you were part of the underground there was no escaping rock – music was a magnet which attracted every talented young adventurer, whatever their profession or tastes. In Leningrad, the best photographers did album covers; artists like Kirill Miller designed the sets; the best designers made costumes; amateur film producers and like the macabre 'Necro-Realists' shot hilarious punk movies. Two of the brightest and most influential figures in the Leningrad counterculture got drawn into the music scene: Sergei Kuryokhin, a pianist and provocateur, started playing in Aquarium, and artist Timur Novikov joined Kino. An ethos of wild punk creativity united art and music.

A structured community of rock fans started to develop – very similar in form to what there was in the West. The amorphous sea of hippiedom was replaced by an archipelago of clearly defined subcultures. Unlike in the West, however, where belonging to one musical tribe or another was often determined by your age, your class or your geographical location, in Russia it was more of a free-for-all. You would see everything everywhere, and if the metalheads were less educated than the hippies, or if the punks were younger than the Russian rockers, then this didn't make itself apparent. Perhaps this is because rock music in Russia never became a nationwide craze, but was always confined to a certain minority residing in big cities, quite well off and with a decent level of education. But this minority was divided into five clearly defined tribes.

Ageing Hippies: They loved classic Western rock and psychedelia and read Carlos Castaneda; their favourite Russian band was Aquarium. A small offshoot of this movement was the 'Russian Rastas'. It's strange but, despite lots of nostalgia for classic Sixties and Seventies rock and the renaissance in vinyl, the hippie movement hasn't ever resurfaced in Russia. But you never know.

Punks: The story of how punk came to the USSR is very similar to what happened with the hippies – it was all because of state propaganda! Like their British counterparts, soviet newspapers loved writing about the Sex Pistols and other scandalous punk groups, casting them both as rebels fighting the 'fascist regime' and as disgustingly dirty hooligans covered in Nazi symbols. It didn't take long for young Soviets to respond to this. As in the West, Russian punk contained a whole spectrum of political beliefs, from anarchists to skinheads, but in Russia the authorities were more worried about the music than the politics. The biggest group was The Automatic Satisfiers from Leningrad, followed by Civil Defence from Siberia. There wasn't much that stood out about their style, except for a penchant for scarves and hats with ear flaps in the winter. Everything else was copied from the Brits, including their symbols and slogans. But the punk bands sang in Russian and they were the first ones in Russia who had the courage to swear, which contributed to their scandalous popularity. When it comes to the music, the only things that I can remember apart

Andrei "Pig" Panov and the group The Automatic Satisfiers, 1988–89. Courtesy of the author

from the endless brutal chords are the extraordinary songs of Siberian punk singer Yanka Dyagileva.

Metalheads: Probably the largest and most solid of the rock subcultures in Russia, based around a shared love for heavy metal and black leather with metal accessories. The music was their passion and metalheads only took a passing interest in politics or art. Inside their own community, the metalheads divided up into a handful of clans – black metal, doom metal, thrash metal, speed metal and so on. They mostly listened to foreign bands from Britain, Scandinavia and America – but they did have Russian favourites such as Black Coffee, Aria and Cruise. If you ask me, none of these bands were that interesting: they played skilfully enough, but the music was standard-issue and the lyrics stupid. In contrast to the Scandinavian 'heathens', Russian heavy metal bands and their fans could not come up with anything frightening, fresh or wild. The biker movement, which shared the metalheads' love of black leather and Motörhead, has now mutated into a patriotic stronghold of Russian Orthodoxy and Putinism.

Yanka Dyagileva, 1989.
Courtesy of the author

Russian Rockers: appearing around the middle of the 1980s, these were the Slavophiles of rock, supporters of indigenous talent who believed that Western rock had died and the new John Lennons and Jim Morrisons were living and playing in Russia. And I agreed with them. Russian Rock fans were the most varied of all and, unlike the other groups, didn't have their own dress code or symbols. Russian Rock's inarguable merit was the magnificent quality of the lyrics, their poetry. If songwriters like Bob Dylan, Jim Morrison and Nick Cave are the exception in the history of global rock music, in Russia the number of rock songwriters who could be published poets is quite significant. One of them, Alexander Bashlachev, is undeniably a genius, a poet on the level of Russian greats like Pushkin or Sergei Yesenin. That said, of course, rock is a lot more than literature set to music, and for the fans the tunes were no less important than the words.

New Romantics: The most vivid but short-lived group – they were fans of new wave, synth-pop and post-punk. They listened to Joy Division, Talking Heads and Ultravox and dressed accordingly. Their favourite Russian groups were Kino and Centre, as well as some ska bands. This was the revival of the spirit of the dandies and the *stilyagi* but now with added eye liner and the occasional zoot suit. Especially notable was the drummer in Kino, Georgy "Gustav" Guryanov, the first person in Russia who had the courage to wear makeup, jewellery and other androgynous accoutrements in public.

Alexander Bashlachev reading the newspaper Soviet Culture, 1985. Courtesy of the author

Over the years I have heard one and the same thing from all sorts of different people – be they famous film producers or half-forgotten punk-poets: that the best period in Russian history was 1985 to 1991, the era of Gorbachev's 'perestroika and glasnost' – restructuring and openness. Why? The answers are predictable. It was a time of profound change, when the country was opening up to the rest of the world and

Михаилъ Сергѣевичъ
ГОРБАЧЕВ

Gorbachev's portrait. Vladislav Mamyshev-Monroe, 1990. Collection of Georgy Guryanov

to a new world of possibility. The shackles of brutality were falling away and ideological dogma crumbling. But this period was unique in another way too: the country and its culture had already been liberated from totalitarianism and censorship, but had not yet fallen hostage to money and the financial markets. So, yes, for people with imagination there never was a more carefree period in Russian history.

It all started very suddenly, in the midst of utter darkness. The Soviet regime could, it seems, have continued to draw out its slow death for a long time, but somehow an instinct of self-preservation was still working among some members of the government elite. Three consecutive General Secretaries of the Communist Party had died in the space of a single year. In April 1985 it was decided to fill that key post with someone younger and not too conservative. What followed is the stuff of history books. I know Mikhail Gorbachev a little and have chatted with him on several occasions in a relaxed atmosphere. One evening, after several glasses of vodka on both sides, I decided to ask him some questions which have always interested me. "Mikhail Sergeevich," I said, "When you launched your perestroika campaign, did you have a clear vision for what you wanted to achieve and a definite plan for how to implement it?" "A vision? Certainly – democratic socialism with an efficient economy. As for a plan, basically there was no precise plan." "But, in 1985, did you have any idea what these reforms would lead to?" This was a question he found a little harder to answer. I think we managed to slip another glass of vodka in. His eventual answer was: "No." A third question was begging to be asked: did the former General Secretary and President of the USSR regret what happened next? But I didn't ask him. Not because I was being polite, but because I know for myself that everything that happened next was for the best. To give Gorbachev his due, he did not follow the traditional path of Russian and Soviet leaders: he allowed the social, political and cultural development of the country to happen freely and naturally. He did not resort to brutality and he didn't substitute democracy with palace intrigues. And although this might sound strange to us now, this was a political leader who was not corrupt, not a thief.

The young people of the USSR gained a lot from perestroika – access to a whole world of formerly forbidden fruit. Everything that had been forbidden for decades was now permitted and the people who had been keeping everything under lock and key just disappeared. The Komsomol, for example, had virtually ceased to exist by the end of the decade. Now you could earn money through small businesses and listen to your favourite music on records or in stadiums; you could go abroad (if you had the money); watch pornography and buy fashionable clothes without a problem. And the people who benefited most from the rapid democratisation of everything were those whose years of languishing in the underground had won them a heroic reputation: the rock musicians. In the space of two years their gigs moved from private flats to massive

Gorbachev's portrait.
Vladislav Mamyshev-Monroe, 1990.
Collection of Evgenij Kozlov and
Hannelore Fobo

Gorbachev's portrait.
Vladislav Mamyshev-Monroe, 1990.
Private collection

stadiums. They were constantly on TV and all the unofficial anthems of perestroika – "Changes" by Kino, "Train on Fire" by Aquarium, "Chained Together" by Nautilus Pompilius – were rock songs. Now that the USSR had suddenly become an interesting country and the world was gripped by Gorbymania, we were inundated by music producers from Europe and America, eager to get a piece of these new hot properties – 'perest-rock' and 'glasnost-art'. Non-conformist artists who had only recently been exhibiting in flats, giving their work away for free, were suddenly the subject of a huge auction, held by Sotheby's in Moscow in 1988. The young actress Natalya Negoda, star of *Little Vera*, the first Soviet film to show nudity, was immediately whipped off to Hollywood and appeared in *Playboy*.

I started writing for *Rolling Stone* and *The Face* and presenting programmes on Soviet radio and television, even though back in 1985 I had been on all the blacklists too. It was a dizzying time, a time when nothing was impossible. We had this strange, unprecedented but quite pleasant feeling that we were on the same page as our leaders. We actually liked the government! For me, the perfect symbol of the riot of culture that was perestroika was the Popular Mechanics, a massive music experiment orchestrated by the manic Sergei Kuryokhin. On one stage he brought together rock bands, a military choir, pop stars, folk shamans, jazz improvisers, avant-garde fashion designers, live animals and whatever else came to hand, creating a crazy carnival that could be at once hilarious and sinister. It was a unique experience: something that had never happened before and was never to happen again. And now, remembering those years, I believe it was the only part of my life which you could compare to the Silver Age at the start of the century, both in its historical importance and in the talent of the astounding individuals who were a part of it.

It was not the young people of Russia who made perestroika happen. Perestroika came from above and continued, mostly thanks to the efforts of the ageing alumni of the Soviet Sixties – the generation of the Twentieth Congress whose revolution had been postponed. Many of them had returned from emigration or from exile. Some of them became members of Parliament, top bosses, editors-in-chief or university rectors.

Meanwhile, the young people were getting on with their own thing – you've got to strike while the iron is hot! Komsomol bosses mutated into businessmen, artists reaped the fruits of their underground fame and ordinary young men and women were free to enjoy life without fear of being expelled from the Komsomol. I can't think of any significant youth movement which emerged at this time, whether in support of or against Gorbachev, either formal or informal. There was a popular programme on TV called *Viewpoint,* hosted by three dynamic presenters in their early twenties, but that was about it. I went to endless anti-Communist demonstrations in Moscow in 1989 and I am witness to the fact that most of the participants were old or middle-aged. (It was a different situation on the periphery of the USSR, particularly in the Baltic republics:

Sergey Kuryokhin, 1992.
Courtesy of the author

Still from the concert Popular Mechanics, 1988. Courtesy of the author

VIKTOR TSOI
(1962–1990)

Russian Rock's greatest icon was born in Leningrad to a Russian mother and Korean father. He became famous as the frontman and lyricist of Kino, who combined a post-punk sound with a New Romantic look and simple, memorable songs full of movement and striving (one of their most famous was the anthemic "We Want Changes"). Their enormous popularity was cut short when, just months after playing to a hundred thousand people, Tsoi was killed in a car accident in August 1990. Nevertheless, Kino's music and Tsoi's image remain unprecedented and unsurpassed in popularity and influence in Russian music culture.

Georgy Guryanov and Viktor Tsoi, late 1980s.
Courtesy of the author

there, young people took an active part in campaigning for national independence.) I guess this is because kids of the Eighties Generation were the descendants of the pagans, not the heretics. (Bashlachev even sang: "Rock and roll – what a glorious paganism!") Politics and ideology were completely foreign to them. Words like 'democracy' didn't feature in young people's everyday lexicon, let alone 'pluralism', 'liberalism' or 'reform'. But young people were responsible for providing the cultural and emotional underpinning of perestroika. Our favourite songs – "Out of Control" by Television, "From Now on We Are in Charge" by Kino and "Revolution" by DDT – remain among the most striking monuments to this magnificent five-year period.

> We step onto the half-built bridge,
> We've put our trust in the stars,
> And everyone shouts "I'm ready!"
> ...We go forward, we're strong and happy,
> Frozen fingers break the matches,
> With which we'll light the fires...

These lines come from a song by Tsoi written in 1986. That bridge remains unfinished and others have fallen down. The fires flared up, but after five years they were extinguished. Still, remembering those happy years, I can't help but recall another line, some two hundred years old, from the Russian poet Vasily Zhukovsky: "Do not grieve that they are gone / Give thanks that they were there at all."

And now, towards the end of this meandering chapter, we must turn off the high road of Russian cultural history onto one of the side paths. We have been spoiled so far by the fact that most of the youth movements under discussion – well, except for the Komsomol, of course – were progressive, freedom-loving and generous, populated by enlightened, creative young people. So it was in Russia – until the late 1970s. It was at around this time, at first in Moscow and the surrounding area and then in other cities and towns, that a much less attractive subcultural energy emerged. The underlying social cause is a familiar one: kids had a bit of money, which meant they were more independent from their parents and had the freedom to choose their own leisure activities. This happened first among the well-off children of the intelligentsia – the *stilyagi*, beatniks and hippies – and then it spread to the poorer outlying areas.

The first, shocking, evidence of this new trend was the emergence of Russia's take on football hooliganism. Traditionally, watching football had been a pretty respectable pastime in the Soviet Union – not exactly a trip to the theatre, but not far off. But suddenly some fans – at first only a couple of hundred – started turning up to away games in organised groups, wearing their team's colours and causing trouble outside the stadiums. While at first this practice came under attack in the press and from the

Lyubery, 1980s.

A *lyubery* badge

KGB, in the late 1980s official counter-measures were stopped and the clubs started to encourage these fans, in part for commercial reasons. The supporters became more and more violent, climaxing in a street fight in Kiev between fans of Spartak Moscow and local team Dinamo. The hooligans never really turned their attention to anyone but rival firms; they tended to get on well with other subcultures, especially the punks, who shared their love of all things English.

Other inhabitants of the city's fringes took up more exotic and more unpleasant activities. In the last years of the 1970s, lots of sports facilities were built in and around Moscow in preparation for the Olympics. Several weight-lifting centres were constructed in industrial areas and in particular in the rough town of Lyubertsy outside of Moscow. Local teenagers, who had nothing else to do in their grim, small-town existence, developed a passion for pumping iron. At first their parents and the police were delighted at this healthy new pastime and the reduction in drunkenness and hooliganism. But soon the obvious question arose: what were these young men going do with those big muscles now the Olympics was over and only a chosen few could ever become professional sportsmen? Soon, small gangs of *'lyubery'*, so called in honour of their hometown, started travelling by train to neighbouring Moscow with only one goal – to punish anyone they didn't like the look of. The *lyubery's* targets were mainly teenagers from intelligentsia subcultures like metalheads, punks and hippies, who stood out for how they dressed. The *lyubery*, unlike the Komsomol, didn't force these non conformists to shave their heads or cut their trousers; instead, they would just beat them up so viciously that some of their victims died.

The *lyubery* had their own dress code – not exactly elegant, but effective. They wore broad, thick trousers with metal inserts sewn into the knees (which helped in fights), caps (replaced by knitted hats in winter), white scarves and leather jackets. What's more, they worked out a mini-ideology for themselves: they described the beating up of subculture kids as a 'purge' or 'renovation' and claimed to be fighting Western decadence and other alien non-Russian influences. They had their own anthem, which began: "We are the sons of Lyubertsy, the home of brutal strength". Here are some of the other lyrics:

You may be black as anthracite,
But you can't hide at night
To all of you getting a free ride
We are bringing genocide.

This is the text, pretty much verbatim, though I doubt any of the *lyubery* knew exactly what "genocide" actually meant. Back in the 1980s people thought the *lyubery* were motivated by a mixture of eagerness for a scrap and a jealous, class-driven dislike of rich city kids. Nowadays I think a little differently: the biggest driving force for these guys from the wrong side of the tracks was hatred for anything not Russian, anything which seemed to threaten 'our' way of life. This primitive feeling, innocently called 'patriotism' is exactly what contemporary propaganda pushes on people. It worked like this in the 1980s too. Although the police did not only allow the *lyubery* gangs to continue their raids in the very centre of Moscow, they also supported them morally, and possibly financially. The police came from the same class as the *lyubery*, and, as one officer told me, they felt that the *lyubery* were doing a good job keeping the hippies, punks and other "fascist filth" off the streets. Some subculture kids who liked a fight themselves were not intimidated, and in the mid-1980s skirmishes between the *lyubery* and the metalheads and punks became something of an everyday fact of life.

But then the situation started to spin out of control: the *lyubery* would go 'on tour' round Moscow and started turning up in other towns. They would travel up to Leningrad for their 'purges'. The press, now under a more liberal regime, went on the attack, revealing among other things, the *lyubery's* cosy relationship with the Ministry of Internal Affairs. Finally, the carnage began to assume alarming proportions: in the summer of 1988, three thousand *lyubery* and metalheads clashed on the Krymsky Bridge in Moscow and some were killed. As soon as the *lyubery* lost support from above, they faded away very quickly – within a year. Exactly the same thing had happened to the Black Hundreds. But while at the start of century the remnants of that fierce mob were swept away into war and revolution, in the early nineties the *lyubery* melted away to join criminal gangs. But that was in a new decade – and a new country.

Renata Litvinova in Andrey Bartenev's performance Sleeping Beauty. Timur V. Grib, 1996.
Courtesy of the photographer

CHAPTER 9

Capital Reconstruction: Gangsters, Ravers and New Russians. 1991–2000

Everything ended very quickly, almost all at once. The Eighties, perestroika, socialism, the Soviet Union, the Communist Party, the Komsomol, the KGB and the rock group Kino all disappeared, to be replaced by the Russian Federation with Boris Yeltsin at the helm and a capitalist economy predicated on 'shock therapy' – the rapid introduction of a free market, whether we liked it or not. There were tanks in the centre of Moscow and a new boom in criminality. The 1990s were a unique decade, one that stands out starkly from the ordinary course of Russian history. When we look back on that time now, people's views are sharply polarised. Some see it as the most liberal period in Russian history, others as ten years of death and humiliation. We remember it either with dewyeyed adoration or with seething hatred. The contradictory opinions on this decade are undoubtedly shaped by contemporary politics. Putin's propaganda portrays these years as the "Wild Nineties", a time of chaos, violence and anarchy in order to emphasise how Putin himself straightened things out when he succeeded the drunken Yeltsin. The opposition, on the contrary, portray the 1990s as an all too short-lived period of freedom and openness. For most Russians, however, your view of the Nineties is a purely personal matter: it was a decade either of total triumph or of complete failure – irrespective of political orientation. In the West, people often say that if you remember the Sixties, you weren't there. You might be tempted to say the same about the Nineties in Russia. It really was a crazy time. But I was there and, oddly enough, I do remember quite a lot. This was one decade that I understood all too well.

In August 1991 all the underlying tensions of the 1980s had come to a head. Let me just remind you: on 19 August an old guard of generals tried to stage a pro-Communist coup, bring down Gorbachev and Yeltsin and return to the Soviet norms which were quickly becoming a half-forgotten thing of the past. In response, hundreds of thousands of people took to the streets and squares of central Moscow, blockaded the troops and defended the parliament where Yeltsin was holed up. Two days later this swan song of the Soviet regime was effectively over. I was there (I was even given a medal for heroism) and I can say with

'The world is changing'.
Vladimir Bogdanov, 1990s.
Courtesy of The Lumiere
Brothers Center for
Photography, Moscow

no qualms that the night of 19 August 1991, the night when everything was decided, was the best in my whole life. People built barricades, lit bonfires and sang songs; they shared the latest news, welcomed friends and met celebrities. They talked about the future. About 90% of the crowd were young people: everywhere I looked I saw people I knew – musicians, journalists and artists. Everyone's eyes were shining, even in the darkness. Or perhaps they were reflecting the flickering fires. The only tragic event of that night was the death of three young people in a tunnel on one of Moscow's main roads, crushed by tanks. But, above all, the coup inspired an amazing display of courage and solidarity. Where did all that go? It seems to me that those two or three days and nights in August sucked all the energy out of the Russian people – particularly the young – for the next quarter of a century. After that, everything in Russia in the 1990s and beyond was misbegotten, uninspired and mediocre. On the subcultural front, things got off to an interesting, if dispiriting, start. Russian Rock, the movement that had invigorated the previous decade, disintegrated, crippled by four new factors:

- These warriors of the underground underwent an identity crisis: how could you sing about rebellion when suddenly everything was permitted?
- The West lost interest: apart from the occasional debut album being released abroad, the world looked away.
- The general public, especially young women, got bored of intellectual but unsexy Russian rockers: they wanted music they could dance to.
- In 1990 and 1991 many of the scene's key figures either died, like Viktor Tsoi, Mike Naumenko and Alexander Bashlachev, or emigrated.

A new musical genre came to the fore – 'popsa'. These were extremely basic dance songs, recorded on cheap Casio and Yamaha tape recorders. The genre's poster boys were called Tender May, a group of young lads raised together in the same orphanage. No one knew what they looked like because their music was so awful that TV decided not to play it. Their quirky producer created four parallel line-ups that could perform simultaneously all over Russia – to a backing track, of course. It was the dream of manufactured pop success come true, long before Simon Fuller or the *X Factor*. And while young girls went into hysterics at Tender May concerts, the older lads drank vodka to the accompaniment of another new musical genre – Russian 'chanson'. In fact, the only thing new about it was its ridiculous name: these songs had absolutely nothing in common with French chanson. In fact, it was based on the old Russian genre *blatnyak*, ballads sung by thieves and criminals in prison and the gulag, where they got picked up by members of the dissident intelligentsia. In the Soviet Union they had been forbidden; in the new liberal era, this long-cherished culture quickly bubbled to the surface, just as underground rock had in its day. *Blatnyak* was hugely popular in the early 1990s, becoming the soundtrack for a new wave of criminal activity in Russia – of which more later.

It was a foreign import that inspired the third, rather predictable, musical subculture of the period – hip-hop. Unlike rock or disco, this new music took a decade to reach Russian youth: the country's first hip-hop festival took place in the summer of 1990 (I was on the competition jury).

There weren't many rappers (or skaters and break-dancers for that matter) in the country at the time but those that there were certainly managed to cause controversy. The first scandal concerned the group

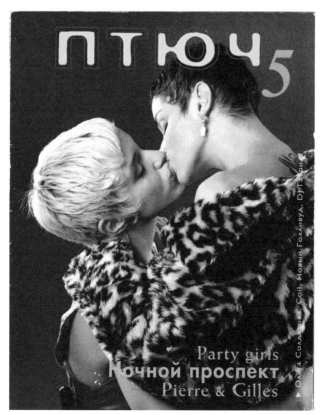

Issues of *Ptyuch* 1995–96.
Courtesy of Igor Shulinsky

Bachelor Party (*Malchishnik*), who were clearly inspired by the Beastie Boys but took things much further. Most of their lyrics were entirely pornographic. Their greatest hits, and in particular the famous "Sex Non-stop" – a cheerful ode to orgies – were played on all the newly liberal Russian radio stations. At the same time, prominent rapper Bogdan Titomir became obsessed with getting across a "positive message" in this time of ideological vacuum and tried to create a sort of youth movement inspired by dance, sport and soft drugs. He was not successful.

If there was a successful youth movement in the 1990s, then it was club culture. It all began in the Leningrad Planetarium, where local DJs and musicians staged electronic raves for small groups of devotees. In 1991 they decided to move this to Moscow and it just exploded. The first big rave was the legendary Gagarin Party, held in the Museum of Space Exploration. It transformed Moscow nightlife. This was what the young and happening crowd in Russia had been looking for: techno and drugs, in abundance!

The drug situation in Russia at this time had changed dramatically. In the 1970s all drugs except cannabis were considered exotic. But in the 1980s heroin started to be trafficked into Central Asia from Afghanistan thanks to the ongoing war there. In the early 1990s the port of St Petersburg became the largest transit point of cocaine from Colombia into the old world. (Some people believe that it was in this business that important figures in our present government elite acquired their seed capital.) Hard drugs, as well as pills of course, were openly sold in clubs: the toilets were equipped with lockers with simple shelves at a convenient height for snorting lines of cocaine.

Clubs of all sorts started popping up everywhere. There were bohemian cellars with live music, glamorous ballrooms for the children of the elite (often in former Soviet Houses of Culture), and, for the first time in the history of Russia, gay clubs. Here I must make a small but important digression: in the USSR homosexuality was still considered a criminal offence and gay culture was kept very much under wraps – if it existed at all. Disco, for example, was extremely popular in the Soviet Union, but was completely devoid of gay overtones. And it would have been unheard of for a public figure to openly come out as gay – pretty much as it would be today under Putin. It was only in 1993 that the law against 'sodomy' was repealed and the gay community was accepted: gay clubs opened, gay magazines began to be published and conferences on homosexuality were held. One of the clubs, Three Monkeys, was right next door to the local police station. My favourite club was Tam-Tam in St Petersburg, an uncompromising post-punk Babylon where early 1990s group Chimera used to play. In Moscow, the most popular raves were held at the psychedelic Hermitage and the more electronic Ptyuch. Once a month the Ptyuch team, who also produced a magazine that was the bible of young clubbers, played host to a night of madness.

Unfortunately, young techno-enthusiasts were soon pushed to one side and the cost-efficient rave business was completely taken over by the mafia. And I mean mafia in the truest sense of the word: drug dealers, racketeers and murderers. St Petersburger Ivan Salmaksov, a leading figure in the early dance music scene, was murdered. This was the other side of the bright shiny coin of the Nineties: for some, freedom meant the freedom to be violent.

In early 1992 Russia descended into political and economic chaos. A system of what people used to call 'market reforms' was introduced. Not being an economist, I won't go into all the technical details (it was all about liberalising financial controls and ownership) and will focus instead on what it meant for the man in the street. The upside of these reforms was that they inspired a feverish entrepreneurial buzz. Everyone wanted to be a capitalist, and the shops and private stalls were suddenly full of goods. The downside, however, was that far from everyone had a talent for business and most people ended up catastrophically poor. The country was plagued by spiralling inflation and unemployment. Cynical reforms based on social Darwinism put millions of people on the brink of ruin. University professors worked as couriers or sold pies on the streets; yesterday's intelligentsia stood in line at pawn shops; pensioners simply quietly passed away.

Unofficial statistics showed that unemployment among young people was higher than 50%. There were some career opportunities but they were in one rather specific area: crime. The total number of people convicted for various crimes under the age of 30 in Russia from 1990 to 2000 was over five million. And that's only first-time offenders. During the same period, the number of Russians aged 18-24 who committed crimes more than doubled, reaching half a million; there were about a million criminals under thirty. By the mid-1990s, there were around five thousand youth gangs in Russia and it is estimated that at least six million Russians aged 14–29 (about 20% of all young people) were involved in some sort of criminal activity. Hundreds of thousands of them died from drugs, gang warfare and occasional clashes with the police. As I say, these numbers are very approximate – perhaps the reality is even more terrible – but they give some idea of the 'great criminal revolution' of the 1990s. The socio-economic conditions were not much different to South Africa and Venezuela today, or even America at the time of the Great Depression, but they did generate their own specific subcultural nuances.

These young gangsters called themselves the *bratva* (from the word *brat*, meaning brother) and each member was a *bratok* (a little brother, a "bro"). Every *bratva* was controlled by older overlords, called the authorities, godfathers or thieves-in-law. I have always hated criminals and gangsters and, unlike many journalists and celebrities, not to mention Russian politicians, I can't boast any in-depth knowledge of underworld hierarchy, slang or codes. But I saw and heard them all the time – that

#5 from the series Kabul Olympics. Sergey Bratkov & Slava Mogutin, 2001.
Courtesy of Regina Gallery, Moscow

was inevitable – so I'm able to present an objective picture of what they looked like.

How could you spot a *bratok*? At the lower levels, he would have very short hair and tracksuit trousers: hence the nickname of these guys, the *'treniki'*. If he was a bit trendier or more successful, he'd sport a brightly coloured cashmere jacket – these guys were known as 'raspberry jackets'. They all wore lots of bling – massive gold chains with or without a cross round their necks, known as the *tsepura* and big rings on their fingers (*golda*). They loved brands like Adidas and Versace, and the car of choice was a BMW. Music wasn't that important to them: they would pop pills in clubs to the sound of techno and house, or if they were feeling soulful, they would listen to Russian chanson. They hung out with other *bratoks*, and prostitutes – *putany* or *shmary*. They were all very young and very vulgar. They filled their spare time by taking drugs in night clubs, getting drunk in restaurants and partying in saunas and massage parlours. One contradiction that remains a mystery to me is how they combined their copious drug use – heroin for the *treniki* and cocaine for the 'jackets' – with their alleged respect for physical strength and fitness.

Leader of Orekhovskaya gang Sergey Butorin (left) with a member of Medvedkovskaya gang Andrey Pilev (right), 1990s

Researchers into the Russian criminal boom of the 1990s have pointed out various psychological characteristics of the *bratoks* that distinguish them from traditional criminals. Most important was their ruthlessness and brutality, which was often completely unmotivated. Two new words appeared in the Russian language in the 1990s and became very widespread. The first was *'otmorozki'*, meaning drugged-up hooligan criminals who had lost all sense of right and wrong and would kill and maim in cold blood. The second was *'bezpredel'*, which literally means 'without limits', and was used to describe the extreme actions of the *otmorozki*. They might turn up at the home of someone who owed them something to 'punish' him and while there would also kill his family, children and any casual acquaintances that happened to be present. I don't think old school gangsters would have acted this way. Another distinctive characteristic of the new wave of criminality was the prominence of nationalist and religious feelings. Many gangs were formed around ethnicity and there was a sharp divide between the 'Slavs' and the 'Caucasians' (primarily the Chechens). I won't even begin to touch on the question of Russia's relationship with the people of the Caucasus – it is a subject as complex as my knowledge of it is superficial. But I will say that the Slav gangsters were open about their respect for the Russian Orthodox Church. It seems odd, to say the least, that after murdering someone the *bratoks* would go to the priests in their pay to be absolved of their sins. They liked to donate their blood-soaked money to the church. And their graves, following early deaths from shootouts or overdoses, were smothered with crucifixes and angels – as if true saints were buried below.

Bratki from Saratov, 1990s

The third distinguishing characteristic of the new breed of criminal was their passion for luxury. The traditional Russian underworld, especially

Bratki tombstones, 1990s. Untitled (from the Essence Series). Denis Tarasov, 2013. Courtesy of the photographer

its leaders – the so-called 'thieves-in-law' – believed in austerity and abstinence. The ideological confrontation between the new gangsters without limits and the criminal old guard was one of the main reasons for the many bloody underworld showdowns of the 1990s. The *bratoks* were obsessed with expensive clothes, cars, fashionable clubs, drugs, top models, glossy magazines and everything else encapsulated by the blanket term "glamour". The idea of glamour came to typify the most important youth subculture of that decade – the New Russians – who soon eclipsed the uncouth *bratoks*. The term was coined by foreign journalists who watched the endless orgies of rich Russians in Moscow in amazement. Ironically, the phrase was taken up both by the New Russians themselves and by others, who used it as a term of derision. There were many people who hated them – virtually the whole country, in fact – but their scorn for these young upstarts often had a tinge of jealousy and grudging respect.

The New Russians had diverse backgrounds in terms of both class and profession. Having jumped in the blink of an eye from 'developed socialism' to wild capitalism, the country now required a myriad of new institutions and professions, from stock brokers to advertising gurus, from PR consultants to club promoters. No one could really understand where they all came from, but these ambitious, hungry, daring and occasionally talented young sharks formed the nucleus of the New Russians. Orbiting this nucleus there were, on the one hand, a number of relatively refined young *bratoks* – the distinction between the legitimate and criminal worlds in Russia is arbitrary at the best of times, but particularly so in the last 25 years – and, on the other hand, there were the successful young artists, journalists and intellectuals. The closest there is to Western equivalent to the New Russians are yuppies. But these were crazy, extreme yuppies, obsessed not only with forging a career and making money but also with finding ways of burning through that cash as efficiently as possible.

The New Russians' philosophy was simple and boring: militant materialism. They were cool, successful and had fun and they were also incredibly disdainful of 'losers' – people who, unlike them, were unlucky in life. There is a typical joke about two New Russians who meet up and immediately notice that they are both wearing the same tie, obviously from either Cartier or Hermès. One says: "I bought mine in a boutique in Paris for a thousand francs!" The other scornfully replies: "You're such a loser, I bought mine on Rodeo Drive for three thousand dollars!" The funny thing about this joke is that it contains a kernel of truth. Looking chic was incredibly important to most New Russians. Many had come to Moscow from the provinces, and though they may have rented cheap apartments in bad areas, they would be sure to show off their Hugo Boss suit and Rolex and to drive off in a Mercedes Benz 600. Did they have any values apart from success, money and hedonism? I doubt it. They had no leaders as such. Their only role models were glamorous pop stars and their brutal producers. In 2015, amid the gloom of Putin's crackdown on civil liberties, Russia went through a phase of incredible nostalgia for the Nineties. It's not unusual to look back fondly on a time when everything was possible when one is living in a time when everything is forbidden. We had New Russian-themed parties, as well as exhibitions, festivals, TV shows and even pseudo-scientific conferences, all about the Nineties. I myself am considered a 'Nineties icon' – I presented popular TV and radio programmes, edited glossy magazines, worked for fashionable record labels, organised a tour for David Bowie and all sorts of other things – so I am always being asked to explain: what was it really like in "the only truly free decade" in Russia, and how exactly did it contribute to Russian culture? Well, we can have a good laugh about the anarchy caused by the New Russians and all the other pretty insane things that happened back then until we're blue in the face, but what did they actually contribute? All those glamorous music videos, DJs, cheap criminal thrillers, pop songs, kitschy TV shows and low-rent imitations of Lynch and Tarantino can't be considered serious cultural achievements. Fun, maybe, even unique in some sense. Take the new sub-genre of gangster movies – that is, movies made by gangsters, when wealthy *bratoks* hired directors to film screenplays they had written, with their friends and girlfriends in starring roles. This sort of thing is a testament to its era, but you'd hardly call it art.

And so almost nothing of value to posterity emerged from out of the mountain of cocaine and similar substances that was the Nineties.

There were some exceptions, of course, born in the underground, that captured the era's spirit of twisted glamour without becoming vacuous. There was novelist Viktor Pelevin, whose *Generation P*, a tale of advertising and mysticism, dissected a decade of post-modernism and consumerism. Or the artist, impersonator and provocateur Vladik Mamyshev-Monroe — a sort of Russian version of Jeff Koons, Cindy Sherman and Boy George all rolled into one. He had a genius for trash and would dress as Marilyn Monroe on his anarchic homemade television show *Pirate TV*. Or the Necro-Realist Yevgeny Yufit, who made incomprehensible films saturated with black humour and white light — the antidote to the superficial mainstream. A different tack was taken by painters Alexander Vinogradov and Vladimir Dubossarsky whose 'post-glamour' style combined Socialist Realism, Pop Art and satirical humour to skewer the eclectic vulgarity of the epoch. But there wasn't much more than that this turbulent decade left to posterity. Maybe everything was just happening too fast back then, it was too much of a kaleidoscope of colour and cocaine. We were drunk on freedom and high on cash: artists simply couldn't bring themselves to engage in the painstaking work of deep self-reflection. This was culture made at gunpoint — urgent but short-lived. The feeling in the air back then was perhaps best captured by one of the decade's most popular songs by the great Britpop-style band Mumiy Troll:

> Slip away…
> There's a madman in the alley,
> He wants to hang us from a hook,
> The girls have lost their beauty,
> The gangsters are sleeping; the park is full of cars,
> There's just us, a couple of young guys,
> Left waiting to be torn apart.

There's no need to go searching for a deep hidden meaning here — sometimes there is no meaning.

VLADIMIR SOROKIN (b. 1955) AND VIKTOR PELEVIN (b. 1962)

In Russia, a country traditionally obsessed with literature, writers are expected to be the spokesmen of their era. In the 1990s and 2000s the baton was picked up by Vladimir Sorokin and Viktor Pelevin – perhaps not the best, some would say, but undoubtedly the most influential authors of their generation. Both Sorokin, a magnificent stylist with almost prophetic foresight, and Pelevin, a subtle and sarcastic diagnostician of contemporary reality's absurdity, give a better account of Russia's present and future than any political scientist.

Screen shot from the film Spring by Yevgeny Yufit, 1987. Courtesy of the author

"Baby, I'm still in the office." Alexander Vinogradov and Vladimir Dubossarsky. 1996. Courtesy of the artists

After the collapse of the Soviet Union, the Russian Federation became its legal successor, inheriting most of the former's territory, resources and population, as well as its nuclear arsenal and the psychological wounds of a defeated superpower. New leader Boris Yeltsin forced through radical and inconsistent reforms that combined increased liberalism with state capitalism, oligarchic self-enrichment and a mafia state, but did little to strip power from Soviet apparatchiks or the KGB. The logical conclusion of all this – after Yeltsin fired on his own Parliament in 1993, launched a vicious war in Chechnya in 1994 and cheated in the 1996 election – was the appointment of Putin as successor in 1999. Even more tragically, the Russian people lost all faith in words like democracy, liberalism and freedom.

Archive of The Boris Yeltsin Presidential Centre, Yekaterinburg, Russia

Boris Yeltsin's Farewell Speech, 31 December 1999.

Dear Russians, very little time remains to a momentous date in our history. The year 2000 is upon us, a new century, a new millennium.

We have all measured this date against ourselves, working out – first in childhood, then after we grew up – how old we would be in the year 2000, how old our mothers would be, and our children. Back then it seemed such a long way off to the extraordinary New Year. So now the day has come.

Dear friends, my dears, today I am wishing you Happy New Year greetings for the last time. But that is not all. Today I am addressing you for the last time as Russian president. I have made a decision. I have contemplated this long and hard. Today, on the last day of the outgoing century, I am retiring. Many times I have heard it said: Yeltsin will try to hold on to power by any means, he won't hand it over to anyone. That is all lies. That is not the case. I have always said that I would not take a single step away from the constitution, that the Duma elections should take place within the constitutional timescale. This has happened. And likewise, I would have liked the presidential elections to have taken place on schedule in June 2000. That was very important for Russia – we were creating a vital precedent of a civilised, voluntary hand over of power, power from one president of Russia to another, newly elected one. And yet, I have taken a different decision. I am standing down. I am standing down earlier than scheduled. I have realised that I have to do this. Russia must enter the new millennium with new politicians, new faces, new intelligent, strong and energetic people. As for those of us who have been in power for many years, we must go. Seeing with what hope and belief people voted during the Duma elections for a new generation of politicians, I understood that I had achieved the main task in my life. Russia will never return to the past. Russia will now always be moving forward. I must not stand in its way, in the way of the natural progress of history. Why hold on to power for another six months when the country has a strong person, fit to be president, with whom practically all Russians link their hopes for the future today? Why should I stand in his way? Why wait for another six months? No, this is not me, this is not in my character! Today, on this incredibly important day for me, I want to say more personal words than I usually do. I want to ask you for forgiveness. Forgiveness, because many of our hopes have not come true, because what we thought would be easy turned out to be painfully difficult. I ask you to forgive me for not fulfilling some hopes of those people who believed that we would be able to jump from the grey, stagnating, totalitarian past into a bright, rich and civilised future in one go. I myself believed in this. But it could not be done in one fell swoop. In some respects I was too naive. Some of the problems were too complex. We struggled on through mistakes and failures. At this complex time many people experienced upheavals in their lives. But I want you to know that I never said this would be easy. Today it is important for me to tell you the following. I also experienced the pain which each of you experienced. I experienced it in my heart, with sleepless nights, agonising over what needed to be done to ensure that people lived more easily and better, if only a little. I did not have any objective more important than that.

I am leaving. I have done everything I could. I am not leaving because of my health, but because of all the problems taken together. A new generation is taking my place, the generation of those who can do more and do it better.

In accordance with the constitution, as I go into retirement, I have signed a decree entrusting the duties of the president of Russia to Prime Minister Vladimir Vladimirovich Putin. For the next three months, again in accordance with the constitution, he will be head of state. Presidential elections will be held in three months time.

I have always had confidence in the amazing wisdom of Russian citizens. Therefore, I have no doubt what choice you will make at the end of March 2000.

In saying farewell, I wish to say to each of you the following. Be happy. You deserve happiness. You deserve happiness and peace. Happy new year, happy new century, my dear people.

Mitki in MacDonalds. Dmitry Shagin, 2003.
Courtesy of the artist

The menu has replaced
burgers and cola with
Russian dishes *pelmeni* and
kvas. Not for sale, but free.

Patriot Games: Mitki, Gopniks and the New Nationalism. 2000–2010

The rise of criminal capitalism and the emergence of a new, dominant class of ruthless gangsters and arrogant nouveaux riches had a varied effect on the Russian people. The intelligentsia lost their privileges and the working class was transformed from the 'class hegemon' of a socialist superpower to a population of beggars. Of the many frustrated, unemployed young people who had either failed or never even tried to become gangster *bratoks* or New Russians, some emigrated, some went on strike and some voted for the communists. One of the younger generation's more appealing responses to the new era was to join the *mitki*. To explain what this means, we need to go back to the dark days of the early Eighties. In 1984 Vladimir Shinkarev, a 30-year-old artist from Leningrad, wrote a semi-fictional book called *Mitki* about the happy and heartfelt lives of his young drop-out friends. The main character, Dmitry 'Mityok' Shagin, based on a real person of that name, is a naïve painter and out-and-out drunkard. Shinkarev portrays Mityok as someone who fluctuates between "tenderness bordering on idiocy and sentimental dejection". These characteristics are reflected in the childlike style and fairy-tale motifs of the novel. However, the author goes far deeper than this, portraying Mityok's artist friends – the *mitki* – not as a group of artists, but as a fully-fledged subculture. They have their own jargon, their own unique fashion sense (mixing naval uniforms with street-sweeper chic), their own favourite books and films (mostly cheerful Soviet ones), and their own code of conduct (drunken but gallant) and sense of honour. The *mitki* were kind, affectionate, unambitious and passive, a bit like Platon Karataev, the simple soul from Tolstoy's *War and Peace*, but above all like a latter-day version of proper Russian hippies, some twenty years later. Vladimir Shinkarev later said that he had written *Mitki* in the dreary atmosphere of the early 1980s as a sort of catharsis – to "take a breath of happy, fresh air" and to show his friends "how to escape mediocrity and boredom". The book was printed in samizdat in 1985 and went unnoticed: perestroika was just getting started and people were otherwise occupied.

Mitki wearing a "one-for-all" naval shirt. Performance. 2005. Dmitry Shagin private archive

It was only five or six years later that it became a phenomenon among the young bohemians of Russia. Suddenly everyone was wearing stripy blue-and-white jumpers and telling each other sweet little *mitki* stories. Famous musicians, including Boris Grebenshchikov and Andrei Makarevich, became *mitki*, as did many artists and writers. A *mitki* newspaper was launched, *mitki* songs were released and documentary films were shot about the craze. This was more than an artistic fad, it was a whole youth movement with charismatic leaders and disciples and slogans to live by. This was a case where art did not reflect reality but actually created it, as had happened the century before with the nihilists and the superfluous men. Mityok, Shinkaryov's semi-virtual creation, became an unlikely twentieth-century Bazarov.

For all its strangeness, however, the story of the *mitki* had a solid logical foundation in the ideas of selflessness, gentleness and overwhelming love that were the antithesis of the pragmatic and cruel doctrines of the New Russians. "Yes, we are losers," the *mitki* were saying, "We don't have much money, no one is afraid of us and we don't want to be better than anyone else – but we're happy, we love everyone and we feel a lot better than you paranoid predators!" Everything about them, and especially their funny baggy clothes, sent off a message of laid-back brotherhood – and it was pretty convincing.

For all its charisma, moral fortitude and its deep roots in the Russian psyche, however, the sentimental story of the *mitki* came to an end sometime in the mid-1990s. It had got a bit boring for our bohemians and new figures began to dominate the art scene. But the *mitki* brand, these artists in their blue-and-white-striped naval shirts, and the real Mityok Shagin himself, a larger-than-life charmer, never disappeared entirely, lasting into the new millennium. Popular with an arty crowd, politically harmless and with a certain fondness for attention, the *mitki* were something of a godsend for the city authorities in their home city of St Petersburg, who encouraged them in every way, transforming them into something of a cultural tourist attraction. They were even invited to take part in some promotional campaigns for the Kremlin. This was the final straw for the conscientious Shinkarev and he announced the end of this glorious phenomenon of his own making by writing a sad and bitter book in 2010 called *The End of the Mitki*. It concludes with the line: "And what reason do I have, actually, to like the *mitki*? The *mitki* killed my friend." That's not entirely true: Mityok Shagin is still alive. I saw him recently. He was as friendly as ever, but lonely, sad and teetotal.

It was not only the harmless *mitki* who were sickened by the capitalist aggression and neo-liberal dogmas of the early 1990s. The non-conformist mood among young people began to stir up nationalist demons, both on the far-right and the far-left. Take Timur Novikov. He had been a leading figure on the Leningrad art scene in the 1980s, a punk and expressionist, who we last saw collaborating with rockers Kino. In 1991 he founded the New Academy of Fine Arts and adopted a conservative neoclassical style reminiscent of the aesthetics of both Stalinism and the Third Reich. His colleague, the fantastically creative musician Sergei Kuryokhin, went even further and actively supported the National Bolshevik Party, a sort of post-modernist nazi organisation whose ideology somehow combined fascism and communism, with some Russian chauvinism thrown in for good measure. Their slogan was "Russia is everything — the rest is nothing!" The national Bolsheviks, or 'natsbols', attracted another influential figure of the era, Yegor Letov, a legend of Siberian punk and founder of the band Civil Defence.

Kuryokhin and I were friends and we had many passionate arguments about our beliefs. My position was simple: however contemptuous we both were of the bourgeois glamour and liberal vulgarity of modern day Russian society — both on a political and aesthetic level — it was wrong for any intelligent, decent person to leap to the opposite extreme and embrace the prehistoric communists, let alone go beyond the pale and join the fascists. His argument was to try and justify the totalitarian theory, which he saw as romantic, that when it comes to fighting against an evil system the end justifies the means. I would be interested to know what my friend would say now that the rhetoric of the National Bolsheviks has to all intents and purposes become identical to the demagoguery of the state, the embodiment of all the banality and philistinism which Kuryokhin hated so much. But sadly he passed away twenty years ago.

A sense of enormous hostility, founded on a mix of everything from delusions of imperial grandeur to poverty and envy, first took over young radicals, but by the early Noughties it had become the mainstream. The unpleasant mood was captured perfectly in two incredibly popular films by Alexei Balabanov: *Brother* (1997) and *Brother 2* (2000). As with the affable *mitki*, these works of art had a profound influence on everyday life. But *Brother* turned out to have more staying power and we are still seeing its endless sequels in Russia today. The plot draws on many sources, including *Rambo*: after two years in the army, Danila returns home to the bewildering reality of Nineties life – a world of gangsters, prostitutes, drugs, corruption and more. Danila decides to restore order – with a gun. And he is a very good shot. All those who are causing the poor, lost generation of young people like him to suffer – the New Russians, the thieves, the cops, the Chechens and the Ukrainians, the con-men and exploiters – fall victim to his unerring aim. In the second film, set mainly in Chicago, it is the Americans, and especially African-Americans, who come under fire. All the while Danila is as restless as James Dean, as reliable as John Wayne and as naïve as Dostoevsky's "idiot" Prince Myshkin. He shoots anyone who makes a false move, all in the name of his belief that "strength, brother, is in truth." He dresses like a *gopnik* (more of which later) and listens only to Russian rock. Everyone who watched *Brother* absolutely adored Danila. They loved his honesty, his selflessness and his skill. Youngsters from pro-Putin movements have marched down the streets with banners proclaiming: "Danila is our brother, Putin is our president!" When I suggested to the talented director that his film *Brother* might be considered fascist (perhaps I was the first person to do so), Balabanov was so surprised that he didn't know what to say. The virus of nationalism, racism and Nazism spread like a pandemic in the first years of the new century: at the end of the 1990s there were only three mainstream ultra-nationalist political parties (Russian National Unity, the National Bolshevik Party and Vladimir Zhirinovsky's Liberal Democrats Party); by the middle of the 2000s there were a dozen or so. There were various catalysts for this situation: one was the wave of migrants from the impoverished Central Asian republics of the former Soviet union making their way to Russia as it enjoyed relative wealth thanks to soaring oil prices. A second was a series of bloody attacks by Chechen terrorists. A third was the slow but inexorable rise of official imperialist rhetoric that accompanied deteriorating relations with Russia's defiant neighbours – the Baltic states, Georgia and Ukraine. There were various far-right groups around, mostly neo-Nazis and skinheads, like the national socialist society, Schultz 88, Mad Crowd, White society 88, Lincoln 88 and the 'Fighting Organisation of Russia Nationalists' (known as BORN). They

Delegates at the 1st Congress of the Russian National Unity (RNE) movement. 1997. Photograph: Alexander Polyakov / Sputnik. Courtesy of Sputnik

adored Hitler – hence 88, nazi code for "Heil, Hitler" – and murdered with abandon – Asians, blacks, Jews and antifascists. The Nationalist Socialist Society alone killed 27 people in 2008. And they were the only ultras who had any real problems with the authorities – the majority of NSS activists are now either behind bars or were shot. But few other far-right groups have been brought to justice. Members of BORN were responsible for the murder of Moscow lawyer Stanislav Markelov and journalist Anastasia Baburova, but it turned out that they had someone looking out for them in the presidential administration.

Traditional far-right groups were soon joined by nationalist youth groups with an esoteric, occult feel. There were pagans (the Circle of Pagan Tradition, the Union of Communities of Slavic Native Faith and the National Democratic Alliance), Eurasians (like the Eurasian Youth Union, who eagerly proclaim Russia's antipathy to the West) and even a sort of Russian take on the Ku Klux Klan called the Navi society. This varied landscape was topped off by a sprinkling of traditional Black Hundred type groups such as the Orthodox standard-Bearers, The Russians and the Movement against illegal immigration. Their special clothes, rituals and music (heavy metal, naturally) gave them a subcultural feel, but they mostly demonstrate how little things change. It wasn't easy to differentiate a Russian Nazi in the 1990s from a German SS officer in the 1930s: a black pseudo-military uniform, an armband with a swastika-like emblem and a thin tie. Their female equivalents just adapted the uniform with black leather skirts and Doc Martens. It seems that the designers of the Third Reich created the optimal dress code for all fascists, forever. In terms of music, Russian Nazis prefer Germany's Rammstein and Slovenia's Laibach, despite the fact that both these bands appropriate totalitarian clichés with a huge dose of irony. The members of Laibach once told me how at

one of their concerts in Moscow a group of young people in dark suits stood in single file right in front of the stage, every so often throwing their arms out into a Nazi salute.

At the other extreme, logically enough, were the antifa, the anti-fascists, made up of anarchists and extreme left-wing groups. As far as I can make out, there were about as many anti-fascists as there were fascists in the Noughties. There were, however, fewer organisations. The Anarchists formed KRAS-MAT and Autonomous Action, while the communists created Vanguard of Red Youth and Left Front. They combined legal activities such as marches, concerts and pickets with illegal ones like beating up and killing their fascist enemies. Their most notorious demonstration was a flash mob of about two hundred anarchists, anti-fascists and environmentalists who gathered in front of the administrative building in the Moscow suburb of Khimki in 2010. The police ignominiously fled from the jeering mob, who threw paint at the building and smashed its windows. The ideology of young, left-wing Russians at the time was far less exotic than what could be found on the right, and generally resembled leftism elsewhere in the world: social justice, tolerance and a hard line against chauvinism and imperialism. They were hostile to the official Communist Party, whose members held seats in Parliament. They also had their own rock groups – mostly punk and ska. Among other popular elements were: long hair, smoking weed, anarchist-punk t-shirts, trainers and hooded jackets.

With this in mind, you might think that youngsters throughout Russia were seriously interested in politics at the start of the new century, but that wasn't the case at all. All this activity was pretty much restricted to Moscow and St Petersburg and the number of people who were drawn to either the far-left or the far-right probably didn't exceed a couple of thousand.

Political and social problems were of absolutely no interest at all to the vast majority of young Russians. The sky-high price of oil persisted throughout almost the entire first decade of the new millennium, flooding the country with money. Even after this income had been plundered by an orgy of theft and corruption from those at the top, there was still plenty left over to ensure that the majority of people lived an unprecedentedly prosperous life, encouraging a growing middle class. Young people's lives revolved around careers and consumerism. Some nicknamed the young generation '*popsa*' (after the mindless music style), but I prefer to call them 'Generation Nought' – in honour of their decade, the 2000s, and in recognition of the value of their cultural output – zero. They lived a life based around sport and fitness, light alcohol and soft drugs, television and social networks, optimism and mobility. Very few young people in the Noughties were willing or able to escape the Bermuda Triangle of office, mall, nightclub. Even their hobbies were childish: they would stage historic reconstructions and cosplay Japanese anime. They were Tolkien fans, emos, cyber goths and extreme sports enthusiasts. Among the latter, as well as the fairly international gangs of skaters, roofers and parkour runners, it's worth mentioning the purely Russian phenomenon of train-jumping – leaping on top of metro trains. Don't ask me why.

For obvious political reasons, the Noughties are now seen as the Putin era, in the same way as the Nineties were the Yeltsin era. According to government rhetoric, the Nineties was a period of chaos and poverty, and the Putin years a time of order and prosperity. The opposition would counter that the difference between the Nineties was the difference between freedom and the loss of freedom. Personally I'm not inclined to make such a distinction: there were many awful things typical of the Putin regime which began in the 1990s, when Putin himself was already a career politician, including violent crack-downs on any opposition (Yeltsin shelled his own parliament building in 1993), a terrible war (in Chechnya 1994–99), staged elections (1996) and that's not even mentioning all the crime and corruption. Putin came to power through Yeltsin, and so, in effect, the Noughties grew organically out of the Nineties. Differences soon began to appear though and became increasingly stark in the years 2003 and 2004. The president and other former KGB men around him accrued more and more power and influence. After two decades of the unpicking of ideology, the high priests of propaganda again shifted into brainwashing mode – especially when it came to politics and young people. In 2001 a young employee in the Putin administration called Vasily Yakemenko (born in 1971) founded an organisation called 'Walking Together' – a clear attempt to revive the Komsomol. The project failed. The name was mocked and its biggest campaign – the public burning of 'harmful' literature, including popular novels by beloved authors Pelevin and Vladimir Sorokin – was even criticised by the politically loyal media. Three years later, this same indefatigable functionary initiated another 'youth movement' – this time under the laconic title 'Nashi' – 'ours'. The movement aimed, among other things, to: "eradicate oligarchs and anti-Semites, Nazis and liberals" – just to make sure no one got left out, I suppose. In practice, all these artificial Putin youth movements were too cowardly and too unpopular to eliminate even minor drug dealers. On one occasion in 2007 they attacked the Estonian ambassador Marina Kaljurand, but on the whole they restricted their activities to attending public demonstrations and patriotic summer camps, smiling happily and wearing t-shirts with pictures of Putin on them. I once had a conversation with a functionary from Nashi. He was no fool and an ambitious lad, from Siberia I think, and when I asked him outright why he'd got himself involved in this organisation he replied with simple cynicism: "There was no other way I could make a career and move to Moscow." During the brief presidency of Dmitry Medvedev (2008–12) Nashi quickly began to falter: the new, more modern leadership obviously did not look favourably on this rather ugly mutation of the Komsomol. It turned out that the state budget for these 'kids' was at least 450 million roubles over a period of four years. Its founder and chief ideologist Yakemenko was accused of paedophilia and Nashi were forced to cut back on most of their political programmes and top staff. Soon they disappeared into the abyss, like all their predecessors.

One of the most popular derogatory nicknames of the presidential youth movement – apart from 'Nashists' and the 'Putin Youth' – was "the raging gopniks". I first heard the word gopnik in 1984 in a great song by Mike Naumenko, called, simply, Gopniks.

Gopniks, 2000s

Who's that in the summer knocking back port?
Who's that in the winter not drinking beer warm?
Who's that who's crapping outside our door?
Who's that who's puking in the metro cars?
Who's that who's giving us black eyes?
Who's that jabbing pens in our sides?
It's the gopniks! It's the gopniks!
They just won't leave me be.

(I should point out that in Leningrad at the time it was the done thing to heat your beer slightly in winter.)

There were always lots of gopniks around, although then we called them 'shpana'. I got into fights with them when I was still a school kid. They were stupid, badly educated, aggressive, often drunk and they hated anyone different from them. It was from the ranks of the gopniks that the hooligans and the lyubery came. In the Nineties they were cannon fodder for the criminality boom. But it was only in the Noughties that the gopniks finally got not only a new name but also a new sense of

A Lad with Pigeons. Ivan Semesyuk, 2008.
Courtesy of the artist

community. They thought of themselves as a subculture, although they didn't feel that comfortable with the word 'culture'. They felt a strange strength rising within them and became increasingly bold. They changed from persecuted young cast-offs to the bosses of their 'hood'. Why? Well, to start off with, there was growing prosperity – now you could not only buy cigarettes and beer, but drugs and a gun too. Secondly, and this is just my guess, this was just the zeitgeist: Putin was a typical Leningrad *gopnik* of the type that Mike Naumenko had sung about – ugly, angry and born resentful. And so it was hardly surprising that in 2004 the third largest political party in Russia, Vladimir Zhirinovsky's 'Liberal Democratic Party', tried to make the *gopniks* their key demographic, signing up new members at railway stations and putting up Zhirinovsky's bodyguard as a presidential candidate. In fact, it was a smart decision: *gopniks* probably made up about a quarter of the young Russian electorate at the time. Though I can't really see any of them going out to vote. The *gopnik* lifestyle could be defined as one of aggressive laziness. They sit around together in the city squares, or by metro stations and bus stops, squatting on the ground, drinking, smoking, nibbling on sunflower seeds and abusing passers-by. They prudently choose their victims from among the weak – school kids and solitary pedestrians – and steal money and mobile telephones. For a *gopnik*, who survives on trifles, the most important thing is to humiliate his victim and feel a sense of power over them. They wear tracksuits. They have shaved heads, apart from a fringe or a few spikes on top. They like Russian chanson and Russian rap. They use cheap drugs like glue and Chinese 'smoking mixes'. Female *gopniks* wear heavy make-up. Their values include xenophobia, homophobia, respect for the criminals and prisoners, whose ranks they often end up joining, and a vague fondness for the Orthodox Church. They never call themselves *gopniks*, preferring the term 'lads' often prefixed with the word 'proper'. Unlike the *lyubery*, they don't feel any particular class-based hatred towards other subcultures and aren't interested in fitness. Their front teeth are often missing – either from fights or perhaps from nibbling too many seeds.

At first the *gopniks* were not very likeable but they were quite interesting. They aroused only a feeling of great contempt among progressive young people but eventually they became an object of fun, and then the subject of a sort of creative appropriation. For all their faults, they were not as banal as the *popsa* culture of the majority. Predictably, the *gopnik* subculture gave rise to gop-art, gop-rappers and comedy shows about 'proper lads'. The most famous Russian musical group of the Noughties was Leningrad, who shamelessly exploited this grass-roots *gopnik* energy, with amusing results. This was the most original culture Russia had to offer at the time: apparently there are even *gopnik* imitators in Finland now, making this Russia's second most successful cultural export of the century after the musical duo t.A.T.u.

From the Instagram of
Sergey Shnurov (Shnur), the
leader singer of the band
Leningrad. 2016–17

What exactly was the 'youth culture' of the Noughties? There wasn't one. I cannot recall a decade which was more barren and insignificant than the Noughties. Some exceptions might be the emergence of Russian comics and internet art, and the resurgence of Russian rap in the form of Kasta, Krovostok and Noggano, which fused a native *gopnik / bratok* aesthetic with violent gangsta rap; similarly dark were a new generation of filmmakers like Vasily Sigarev and especially Andrei Zvyagintsev. But for the most part, Russian culture fell further under the globalising spell of the internet and its marketplace of homogenous English-language bands and computer games. And all the while, the general public in Russia would probably rate the country's greatest cultural contribution in this decade its victory in the 2008 Eurovision song contest: *popsa* reigns supreme. It is a cruel paradox that in Russia relative prosperity and stability inevitably lead to boredom and blandness, whereas poverty and instability have a very different effect. To quote the lyrics of Eighties poet-rocker Alexander Bashlachev: "In the morning it's really boring and in the evening it's really scary." And, at the end of the Noughties, evening fell.

Let everyone hear my silence. Radya, 2012, Moscow

CHAPTER 11

No Country For Young Men:
Apathy and Protest. 2010–2016

Francis Fukuyama was wrong about the "end of history" after the collapse of the Soviet Union – both in a global sense and in a more localised one. Nevertheless, just like the West in the 1990s, in Russia in the early years of the twentieth century it seemed like all movement had come to an end and that we had arrived at a sort of status quo – one that was far from ideal but which, with a few exceptions, suited pretty much everyone. Yes, we had an authoritarian regime, only notional democracy and corruption was worse than ever before, but at least people's lives were tolerable. The middle classes now had a guaranteed holiday in Turkey and a new Hyundai. The 'upper middle classes' had an apartment in Spain and a Mercedes-Benz. People working in art and culture enjoyed relative freedom and salaries they previously couldn't have dreamed of. As for young people, all their wildest dreams had come true. They had the internet, sex, drugs, pop culture, high culture, gadgets and as many trips abroad as they wanted. In effect, the authorities had made a secret pact with the general population: if the people closed their eyes to the endless theft and corruption of those in power, then the government would allow them to frolic as they wished, catching crumbs from the master's table. In the language of Putin's slogans, this was called "stability". The only secret protocol of the pact was a small Faustian trick, aimed mainly at businessmen and the artistic intelligentsia, which basically said: "Don't get involved in politics, don't poke your nose into what we're doing." The businessman Mikhail Khodorkovsky paid for breaking this pact with ten years in jail and the journalist Anna Politkovskaya – along with other colleagues of hers – paid with her life.

There were a few groups who opposed the regime, mainly a small coalition of old, liberal dissidents – the last guard of bureaucrats from the Yeltsin era. There was also a small, mainly young, group with either left-wing or ultra-nationalist leanings. The conflict between the opposition and the powers-that-be was mostly formal in character. For example, every 31st of the month (in other words, seven days a year) a rally was held on Triumfalnaya Square in Moscow to celebrate statue 31 of the Russian constitution, which guarantees freedom of assembly. I went to one of these rallies once. Opposition leader Boris Nemtsov, who in 2015 was brutally murdered, dragged me out of my house so I couldn't say no, but it all seemed completely pointless. We found two or three hundred silent protesters standing around on the square, surrounded by hundreds of journalists and about a thousand riot police. The same thing happened every time. Everyone would be standing around on the square and the police would ask them to leave. Around forty minutes later they did. The whole protest involved leaders of the opposition being arrested while photographers took pictures with their flash bulbs. And so it was every single time. But I never went more than that once.

Nevertheless, little by little, there was something going on underneath the surface while we were in the cosy cocoon of "stability". A generation was growing which had never known government oppression. It was the first Russia had ever seen. I started to notice these unusual young men and women at the end of the first decade of this century – among youngsters I knew, including students, musicians and the children of my friends. The first thing that I noticed was that they didn't have the typical Russian hang-ups. As a rule, 'progressive' young Russians have always tried to be like foreigners. In the nineteenth century they tried to be like Europeans, in the twentieth like Americans. But the key word here is 'tried'. All these efforts, some of them very clumsy, simply raised an indulgent smile. But these kids were truly cosmopolitan in a cool and organic way. They weren't exactly proud of Russia, but it wasn't a burden to them either. It was just the place where they happened to live. They communicated with the whole world through the internet and instead of using the money they had saved to buy new expensive clothes, casino chips and cocaine, they flew to London or Berlin where they went to exhibitions, lectures and concerts. On the whole, they valued art – and I mean art, not entertainment – and education. They spoke English fluently and unostentatiously. I would go to small clubs to watch bands like The Jack Wood or Scofferlane, or go to a street art festival or an exhibition of comics in a squat, and I always got the impression that there had been a shift in time and space: it was something like being in Manchester in 1979, or Melbourne in 1981, or perhaps the Lower East Side in New York. Yes, it was fairly derivative, but at the same time it was natural and convincing – these were the real Russian 'westerners' – the dream of the *zapadniki* had come true! I wouldn't say that this was a unified subculture: there were bearded hipsters, street food obsessives and art-house cinema nuts; there were greens, into anything organic and ecological, and geeks with their robots and other futuristic gadgets. I remember being particularly struck by that last group. I was invited to give a lecture at a Geek Picnic in St Petersburg: I spent the whole day wandering around a large park, lined with booths full of computer novelties and gadgets – from steampunk gizmos to Tesla cars. There were about ten thousand young people at the picnic and there was a food court which sold alcohol, but yet I didn't see a single drunk person the whole day. It was shocking. It felt very un-Russian. Perhaps it was just chance that every single well-behaved young person in St Petersburg had gathered in the same place, but it was nevertheless astonishing. What's more, in comparison with the 1990s and early 2000s, the whole scene became much more interesting and diverse. The *bratoks* nearly faded away; cosmopolitan hipsters became the height of fashion; technology became central. But was there anything more to this new generation than just a passion for culture and technology? Had the zeitgeist really changed in time for this second decade of the twenty-first century? I was to get the answer to this question on 22 August 2010. Eco-activists, led by young mother Zhenya Chirikova, held a meeting on Moscow's Pushkin Square to protest against the felling of some ancient oak trees on the outskirts of the city to make way for a highway. The rock singer Yuri Shevchuk had agreed to sing at the meeting and I said I'd go with him. We were expecting a crowd of two or three hundred people. Yuri and I went by subway in case we were detained on the way. As we came out of the subway entrance I simply couldn't believe my eyes – the square was packed with people. There must have been around ten thousand of them, and they stayed for the whole three hours, while we shouted into the megaphone and sang songs. It was the biggest demonstration in Moscow since 1993 and the massive turnout was completely unexpected. I remember shouting at the crowd: "Remember, the first decade is over! A new decade has begun! The last decade was like the Seventies – nothing happened; but what happened after the Seventies? The Eighties! And this new decade will be like the Eighties – everything will change!" (I was presuming, though I wasn't entirely sure, that this was a good thing.)

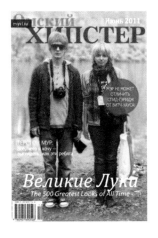

On 11 December that same year, another important protest took place, on a square outside the Kremlin in Moscow, but this one was a lot less peaceful. On the eve of this rally, a fight had broken out in the north of Moscow between Russians and migrants from the Caucasus in which 28-year-old Yegor Sviridov, the ringleader of a group of football fans, had been shot and killed. The police arrested the alleged murderers, but later released them – presumably in exchange for a bribe, as is common practice.

In protest, a group of five thousand well-organised football fans and nationalists gathered under the walls of the Kremlin. There was a skirmish with the police and dozens of people on both sides were injured. In an attempt to calm the crowd, the head of the Moscow police had to promise that the suspects would be arrested again.

Spoof magazine covers: "The Omsk Hipster" and "The Severo-Angarsk Hipster"

A new generation had begun to show their mettle and, having had enough of bread and circuses, it was taking a chance on trying for something more – they wanted respect. The young generation wanted to stand up and be counted.

"You can't even imagine us / You don't even represent us" by Pavel Arseniev.

Protest against results at the parliamentary elections in St Petersburg.
December 10, 2011.
Photograph: ITAR-TASS / Ruslan Shamukov.
Courtesy of ITAR-TASS

The authorities were accustomed to dumb submission and a belief in the inviolability of the 'pact' and so they either didn't notice this new trend, or they underestimated it. On the 24 September 2011 they informed the Russian people that President Medvedev was stepping down to the post of prime minister and that Putin was to become president again. The passive majority had long ago realised that the people in Russia had no voice and so they accepted this news with indifference. However, the active minority (10–15% of the population) were angered and alarmed. Firstly, because the 'reshuffle' was so brazen and cynical and showed not one iota of the respect they had demanded – neither to the people nor the constitution. Secondly, the prospect of having an ageing KGB agent with a *gopnik* attitude as president was vaguely disquieting. The enlightened public was already used to the smiling, iPhone-toting Medvedev, with his incessant droning on about modernisation, and on the whole, he suited them. Soon after, in early December, parliamentary elections were held: the results were clearly rigged in favour of the Putin-Medvedev United Russia Party – and that was when lightning struck! Hundreds of thousands of people poured out onto the streets of Moscow, St Petersburg and other big cities to protest.

These 'New Decembrists' had very varied social and political outlooks. Activists from every end of the opposition spectrum – left-wingers, nationalists, liberals – miraculously rallied together against the despised authorities. However, surprisingly, the vast majority of the protestors were largely apolitical. They were usually described, rather vaguely, as 'the creative classes'. This is perhaps correct, but I'd like to be more specific. At least half of the demonstrators were members of that 'first free generation' I mentioned – hipsters, geeks and other inquiring, progressive minds. It wasn't just their sense of civic responsibility which led them out onto the streets, and their indignation at the dishonest authorities and their reluctance to let Putin back in, but also a fundamental drive: it was now trendy to go out and protest, it was fun, it was creative.

Over the Moscow winter protests became a sort of artistic parade with amusing slogans, handmade placards and even whole portable artworks. The intelligentsia and the middle classes, including businessmen and former New Russians, came out and stood shoulder-to-shoulder with the hipsters. They were probably driven by ideology and pure pragmatism – they feared for Russia's liberal European future. The pro-government mass media wanted to portray a "silent majority" of well-heeled protestors as "infinitely distant from the people" (in the words of Lenin's description of the Decembrists), and so they coined the term "the Mink Opposition" – after the expensive fur coats that they wore to rallies. There was some truth to this. Unlike Occupy Wall Street and the Arab Spring movements that were happening around the same time, the Russian protests of 2011–12 had no economic motivation. Among the many hundreds of banners, I didn't see a single one that mentioned unemployment, redundancies or low wages. It was all about justice, freedom and dignity. All very noble, but was it practical? Perhaps the lack of a 'self-interested' agenda and a disregard for the worries of ordinary people was indeed one of the movement's great weaknesses.

But it was not long before the 'first free generation' and the creatives began to lose momentum – and to a significant extent that was our own fault. In December 2011 the authorities were demoralised and alarmed by the demonstrations. On the 24 December the largest rally yet was held – one hundred thousand people marched to Sakharov Prospect in central Moscow. Towards the end of this giant demonstration, the leaders of the opposition, who were standing on the stage, wished the parting crowds a merry Christmas and a happy New Year and told everyone to enjoy the holidays and to meet up again in February. I swear to God, I couldn't believe my ears. What? I rushed up to the leaders of the meeting (I was also speaking at the rally and had been standing in the wings) and said: "What the hell do you mean – February? We're just starting to pick up momentum here and we need to strike while the iron is hot. We need to go and seize the Central Election Committee building and recount the fake results of the elections! And then we'll be right by the Kremlin itself!" They replied without a shadow of embarrassment or remorse: "Listen, old fellow, I'm flying to the States tomorrow." Or: "Nah... I'm off to Dubai for the New Year..." and so it went on. And then I understood that the revolution had, at the very least, been postponed, but more likely than not it had been called off altogether, and all because its self-proclaimed leaders took such a frivolous attitude towards it.

You might say that the middle-aged leaders had betrayed the radical youth. To these die-hard liberals 'revolution' sounded like a swearword and, just as the Soviet dissidents were always citing the Soviet constitution, so the new opposition leaders were desperately afraid of going beyond legal methods of opposition – legal as defined by an authoritarian government. Yes, they were a boring lot. The young people may have been a bit livelier, but they were just as helpless and childish too: their attitude to the protest was "we had a great time, we stuck it to the government for a while, and now it's time to go home". There was no question of any more serious intentions; we would only see serious intentions from protestors in 2013–14, but that was in Kiev on the Maidan. A few more small 'creative' protests took place, but nothing really concrete. And so, in that same Central Elections Building, Putin swept to victory in the presidential elections. The day before his inauguration, on 6 May 2012, 20,000 or so people, mostly young, came out onto Bolotnaya Square in Moscow. But the authorities were not what they had been six months previously. They had gotten smarter and tougher. The demonstrators were met with armed riot police and brutally beaten and arrested. Many were later tried and imprisoned for "resisting the police". The myth was dispelled that protest marches were a walk in the park and that the government could be changed without violence. And from that moment on, the protest movement began to fade away.

Everything that has happened, and is happening, in Russia from 2012 onwards can be described in the simple phrase 'from bad to worse'. The screws of political repression were tightened and freedom of expression was curbed. Imperialist nationalism and orthodox obscurantism became state policy. Xenophobia, homophobia and the cult of Putin's personality became a daily way of life. And of course corruption, thievery, selective justice and incompetent management was still rife. Perhaps the best way to describe the atmosphere in the second decade of this century in Russia would be Hunter S. Thompson's "fear and loathing". If the Nineties were a time of recklessness and excitement, and the Noughties one of plenty and of boredom, then in this current decade, for the first time in thirty years, the country has reverted back to timid hopelessness. It is true that there was a brief spark of euphoria when the Crimea was annexed, but the general mood was without doubt one of uncertainty and depression. There is nothing left of Putin's stability but Putin himself.

Young people within this new paradigm have started to look pretty pathetic: not exactly lost or in hiding (though they are perhaps both of these things) but hardly noticeable. Apart from a few heroic exceptions – which I will return to shortly – the younger generation in Russia are no longer making the headlines. Now the news is all about the military, about strikes by long-distance truckers, about cynical media-vampires and idiotic parliamentary deputies – but none of them are young. Was there a massive anti-war movement in connection with the aggression in Ukraine? Unfortunately not. In fact, quite the opposite. Hundreds of radically-minded far-right and far-left mercenaries and volunteers went off to fight against their new enemy, the Ukrainians. Even the *Nashi* movement and other pro-Putin youth groups, who had been so vociferous before, have fallen silent. Obviously, the recession and cost of the wars depleted the financial support they received from state coffers. The only headlines

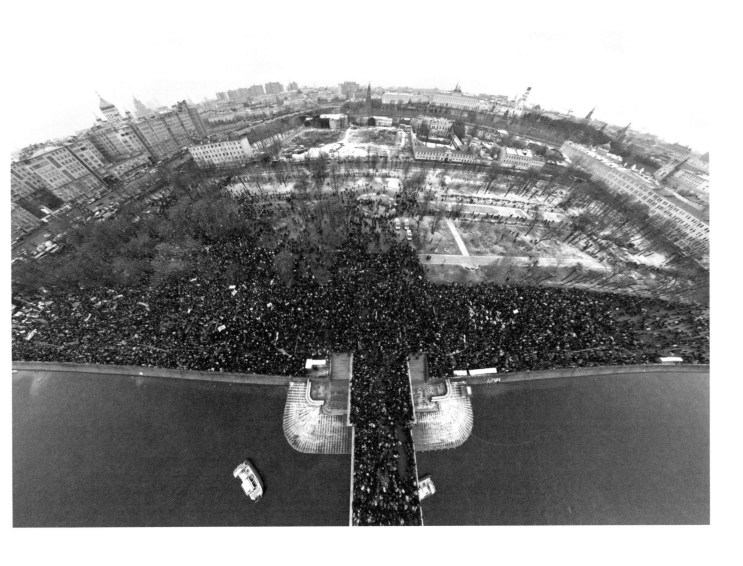

Meeting on Bolotnaya Square, 2012. Project AirPano.
Courtesy of Sergey Rumyantsev

Clothes for a Demonstration against the Faked Election of Vladimir Putin, 2011–2015.
Gluklya's (Natalia Pershina-Yakimanskaya). Installation. 56th Venice Biennial, 2015.
Courtesy of the artist and AKINCI, Amsterdam

about youngsters in recent times have concerned the suicide of 18-year-old Vlad Kolesnikov, who was bullied by his peers for his "political non-conformism" and particularly his opposition to Russian intervention in Ukraine, and who received no protection – in fact quite the opposite – from the authorities. From reading articles about him, I discovered that Russia has a higher teenage suicide rate than any other European country, the fourth highest in the world. To paraphrase the title of the Coen brothers' film, Russia has become no country for young men. And this is no coincidence, but rather the result of a specific government policy that can be summarised with the nihilistic punk motto: "No future".

There is a popular cliché that Putin's Russia is a revival of the USSR. This is true as far as imperialist ambitions and a return to totalitarianism is concerned. But in one respect the situation in Russia is very different: the Soviet Union as a country was all about the future. A future, which was bright, communist and better than the present. The future was a fetish, an obsession for young people. Hence the Komsomol and its creative enthusiasm, the cult of education and the space programme. Today's Russia, on the contrary, is a country which only looks to the past.

This is quite logical because our feudal economic and political system brings with it medieval values: the adoration of great warriors and tyrants (primarily Stalin); the sacred cult of past victories; fanatic Orthodoxy; in-tolerance of heresies and any other deviations from the norm; a disdain, if not phobia, for science and education; suspicion and hostility towards anything 'foreign'; and a siege mentality. In Vladimir Sorokin's book *Day of the Oprichnik* – which I heartily recommend – he describes Russia at the end of the twenty-first century as being exactly like the medieval kingdom of Ivan the Terrible, but with limousines and mobile phones. This satirical dystopian tale appeared in 2006 but has proved prophetic in many ways. A foreign tourist visiting Russia for a week, going to see the Hermitage and Red Square and popping into McDonalds, Zara and the Hyatt Regency along the way, might think I'm exaggerating, but unfortunately I'm not. I would say that in today's Russia the things that have always defined the mentality of young people around the world – independence, curiosity, openness – are somehow… inappropriate.

Thoughtful young people in Russia don't have many options left. The most popular response to this has been emigration. A few years ago there was even a new word for it – *poravalism*, from the phrase *'pora valit'*, which roughly means 'time to get out of here'. I conducted my own mini-survey among nineteen children of my friends, aged between 16 and 28. Only four of them wanted to stay in Russia; the other fifteen had either already left or were seriously thinking of doing so. These results are, I think, representative of the opinions of educated, opposition-minded young people. Although I myself never wanted to emigrate from the USSR (I found it interesting), I do understand the young men and women

Pushkin Square, 9 May 2012

Veteran: "We defended the Motherland!"
Riot Cop: "And we are mopping up the square"

Drawing from A Chronicle of Resistance. Victoria Lomasko, 2011–2012.
Courtesy of the artist

of today: if you're smart and you don't want to be a thief or a government thug– or their victim – there is nothing for you to do in this country. The other option is 'internal emigration'. It is not as popular as it was in the 1970s and 1980s: for a start, the borders are still open, and secondly – this is a bit difficult to describe – I would say that artistic autonomy was more attractive in the Soviet era, when all things Western were the forbidden fruit of freedom but didn't yet have a bitter aftertaste.

Nevertheless, a new underground is growing fast – especially in the provinces. This is another reason for the wave of Nineties nostalgia, for the renaissance in *kvartirniki*, private lectures and salons. Small theatres have sprung up and the old highbrow tradition of poetry evenings has been revived. Young rock bands – and this is something I'm particularly pleased about – have remembered their mother tongue and started to sing songs about real life. The best thing that has happened to young people in Russia in recent years has been the volunteering movement. The recent Nobel Prize winner Svetlana Alexievich said in an interview: "We placed all our hopes in the 'first free generation'. But in 2011 they went out to Bolotnaya Square and the government dealt with them brutally. All that was left of their passion and drive went into volunteering." There is volunteering all over the world, of course. There are no fundamental differences in volunteering between Russia and the West, but there are a few intriguing nuances. The movement, which had limped on from the 1980s into the 1990s, has in recent years, quite spontaneously, grown massively in scale. This wasn't driven either by a thirst for adventure and altruism, but rather because of the total inadequacy and inactivity of the government. The first major outbreak of enthusiasm for volunteering came in the hot summer of 2010 when forest fires broke out across Russia. The failings of the local authorities drove thousands of city youngsters out to help in the villages. Two years later there was a terrible flood in the Kuban region of southern Russia and around 2,500 volunteer rescue workers from all over the country went to help out. Incidentally, the local authorities were again criticised because they didn't warn the residents of the impending disaster and quietly deserted the flooded areas.

The state's attitude to the volunteers was mixed: of course, they couldn't criticise them, let alone put a stop to their noble endeavours, but the bureaucrats' first instinct was to see them as the enemy because they were acting independently from the state. Naturally, therefore, attempts were made to control the volunteer movement: laws were put in place and artificial organisations and umbrella structures were created. For example, at the 2014 Winter Olympic Games in Sochi, 25,000 volunteers (instead of the planned 75,000) were mobilised to help out. Nevertheless, the volunteer movement is still pretty much self-governing and is allowed to be so, as long as it remains politically neutral, which you would expect anyway from things like rescue operations after natural disasters, helping the disabled, the ill and orphans, searching for missing persons and protecting the environment and animals. Are volunteers real agents of change in Russia today? Obviously the country gets more out of them than they do from the wave of emigrations, but whether or not these hundreds of 'small deeds' can come together to create one or two big changes is, at present, difficult to say.

The volunteering movement has effectively almost become a subculture in its own right – a sort of subculture of good intentions – made up of volunteers and charities of all sorts, devoted to saving anything from the environment to historical monuments. The emergence of this group has been part of a wider shift in the culture towards greater diversity and polarisation. Conformist pro-government movements (*Nashi* and the like) have become increasingly confrontational and insistently patriotic, not least in the resurgence of so-called Cossacks, all handily funded by central government. Meanwhile, the economic crisis has put paid to any sense of hedonism and the political mood has exacerbated the desire for escaping into the digital space of computer games and social networks. Islamic groups have become more hardline and more isolated; at the same time fundamentalist Orthodox groups, like those around the 27-year-old Dmitry Enteo, have taken on new visibility and influence, especially in the atmosphere of patriotic fervour caused by the war in Ukraine. Only the freedom-lovers close to my heart have had their ranks severely depleted by arrests, intimidation and forced emigration.

The last time I was at an opposition rally on 20 September 2015. It was in the Moscow suburb of Marino and was attended by around ten

Pussy Riot action at Lobnoe Place on Red Square. Denis Sinyakov, 2012. Courtesy of the photographer

thousand people. They were lovely, kind and smiling, possibly the best people in Moscow. Around half of them were young: hackers from Alexei Navalny's anti-corruption foundation, campaigners on behalf of political prisoners, 'anonymous internet users' with a political bent. Not a lot of people, it must be said – and hardly any public figures, apart from me, an 'aging bon vivant' and long-forgotten TV star, who was all constantly stopped and thanked for just being there. Younger celebrities seem to be determinedly unpolitical. There is one group, however, that have successfully combined global fame with a radical political agenda. You might have heard of them: Pussy Riot.

Pussy Riot emerged in 2011 from within the radical art collective Voina (meaning 'war'). Founded in 2007 by Oleg Vorotnikov, Natalia Sokol, Leonid Nikolayev and Alexei Plutser-Sarno, among others, Voina made a name for itself by staging provocative and politically subversive performances. This same flair for striking often humorous getsures was inherited by Pussy Riot, which was started by Voina members Masha Alekhina, Nadia Tolokonnikova and Katya Samutsevich as a concept-driven punk band with a militant feminist agenda and a Riot Grrrl aesthetic. Their first important action took place on Red Square on 20 January 2012: eight young women stood on the square in balaclavas, at the place where in former centuries the tsars' decrees had been announced to the people, and sang a song entitled "Revolt in Russia – Putin Pees his Pants!". For me, it was their most effective protest. On 21 February Pussy Riot tried to sing their new song "Virgin Mary – Get Rid of Putin!" in Moscow's biggest church, the Cathedral of Christ the Saviour (now better known around the world as the Pussy Riot Church), but were stopped by security guards. Alyokhina, Tolokonnikova and Samutsevich were arrested and, after a series of laughable court cases in August 2012, the first two were sentenced to two years' imprisonment – a decision which was welcomed by Putin. Their story had huge resonance in the West and was supported by many celebrities, including Paul McCartney and Madonna. This made Masha and Nadia the most popular Russians around the world since the time of Gorbachev. But as with Gorby, acclaim abroad translated into a chilly reception in their homeland. Even opposition groups were divided in their opinion of Pussy Riot's 'punk prayer' and the music and art communities gave them absolutely no support at all – I suspect this was just sour grapes at the instant fame achieved by these upstarts, even if they had ended up behind bars. Towards the end of 2013, in the run-up to the Sochi Winter Olympics, Masha and Nadia were released under an amnesty and now they divide their time between rock and roll in the West and human rights work back home. I hope they'll show us yet again what they are capable of.

Another important exception to the rather depressing quiet of recent years has been the 32-year-old performance artist Pyotr Pavlensky. The first of his famous acts of artistic protest was *Seam*, in the summer of 2012:

as a gesture of support for Pussy Riot, Pavlensky sewed his mouth shut
with coarse thread and stood in lone protest outside the Kazan Cathedral
in St Petersburg. He cited as a motivation for the act the complete
indifference to the fate of Pussy Riot among the Russian art community.
In his second performance, *Carcass*, the naked artist wrapped himself in
coils of barbed wire and lay at the entrance to the Legislative Assembly in
St Petersburg. "The human body is as bare as a carcass," he said, "covered
by nothing except barbed wire, which was created to keep livestock in…
This barbed wire pen of mine is a metaphor for the persecution of the
6 May prisoners [those arrested for the protest on Bolotnaya square]
and state repression." His third and most difficult protest was *Fixation*.
Pavlensky stripped naked on Red Square and drove a large nail through
his scrotum into the ground. "The naked artist," he later said, "looking
down at his testicles nailed to the cobbles is a metaphor for the apathy,
political indifference and fatalism of modern Russian society." It's hardly
surprising that after every performance, Pavlensky has been sent for a
compulsory psychiatric examination, but every time the doctors found
him to be sane. (I have known Pyotr and his lovely family for years, and I
can confirm that I have met few more normal and conscientious people in
my life.) He protested against his enforced psychiatric incarceration with
another performance, *Segregation*, in which he cut off his ear lobe. Prior to
that, in 2014, he staged his only "positive" happening – *Freedom* – a sort
of 'micro-Maidan' protest in support of Ukraine outside the Church of the

Gagarin. Crucifixion.
Alexander Zhunev, 2015.
Courtesy of the artist

Spilled Blood in St Petersburg with drums, burning tyres and anarchist and Ukrainian flags. "The struggle against imperial chauvinism continues at the Church of the Spilled Blood," his statement at the time read. "This was the place where the tsar was assassinated by the People's Will and where political uprisings were brutally suppressed. We call on everyone to come out on the Maidan festival day to stand up for their freedom. Bridges are burning and there is no way back."

This last phrase could be applied to Pavlensky's most recent and most important protest. On 9 November 2015 he poured petrol round the wooden entrance of the FSB headquarters in Moscow (formerly the home of the KGB) set fire to it and then stood at the burning "Gates of Hell", as he called them, waiting to be arrested. The photograph of the artist standing in front of the flames with a petrol can in his hand is incredibly powerful. In my humble view, this image is the best to have come from a Russian artist since the time of Futurists. Pavlensky was arrested after thirty seconds. Not one of Russia's opposition leaders expressed their solidarity with the actions of Pavlensky and Pussy Riot – either they weren't to their taste, or, more likely, they didn't want to associate themselves with someone voters might consider crazy. There is nothing too tragic about this since absolutely no one in Russia puts any faith in politicians anyway: even the most radical ones are hardly calling for people to mount the barricades and, of course, no one believes in elections. Hence we are left guessing: will we carry on slowly rotting, will there be a coup, or perhaps some kind of 'black swan' event will fly into view? Driven to speculation by hopelessness, I have developed my own theory of a thirty-year cycle in recent Russian history. The 1950s and the 1980s both started terribly – Stalin in the 1950s, Brezhnev and the Afghan War in the 1980s – but ended on an inspirational high – the Thaw and perestroika respectively. The 1990s mirrored the 1960s: a wonderful beginning – Gagarin, the overturning of the 1991 putsch – followed by a grim conclusion – the crushing of the Prague Spring, the emergence of Putin. In the 1970s absolutely nothing happened, just like the 2000s. With this premise in mind, the current decade should, therefore, most resemble the 1950s and 1980s. Where is our 20th Congress, our secret speech? Where is our glasnost, our perestroika? I don't know. A new military unit has been created, the National Guard, and it is bristling with hostility to any thought of change; a few brave artist-activists have stepped out into the fray; volunteers have gone around collecting medicine; the hipsters have put in their headphones; the revolutionary hackers have opened their laptops; the anarchists have unfurled their banners; the *gopniks* have taken another swig. And, a century on from 1917, we might just be witnessing the beginning of a new era.

Threat. Pyotr Pavlensky, 2015. Courtesy of the artist

Protests in Moscow. George Malets, 2017. Courtesy of the photographer

Starting Over

I have two wonderful young friends, a husband and wife called Max and Natasha. They're about thirty years old. Max used to work as an executive in a big company but, like any normal person would, he got bored of that. He decided to swap suits for baseball caps, grow a beard and start making the best burgers in town. He opened a street-food stall, then another, and now he has his own restaurant in a basement in one of the hippest areas of Moscow. Natasha, a former model, owns a successful boutique around the corner where she sells clothes made by avant-garde British designers. They went to all the protests a few years ago and they harbour no illusions about Putin's power and its consequences. And they're not short of problems either: the bank that Natasha used to keep her money in suddenly failed one day; Max, no doubt, has to be pretty nimble in his dealings with the local bosses, both legal and illegal. You could say that, for them, the outlook is uncertain at best. But still, they live a happy life, they travel, they throw parties, they look after their kids. When asked the obvious question – don't you want to emigrate? – Max just shrugs and, with a slightly guilty smile, says: "Oh no… for now… we're… sort of… staying." Do I see in these two typical representatives of enlightened urban living any 'revolutionary potential'? Not really. Do I see in them some possible foundation for a normal, honest, intelligent life in Russia in the future? Without a doubt. And not just in them.

Observing life here over the last few years has a surreal effect on you, one that's not so much psychedelic as schizophrenic. There are all the stupid mantras about Russia's unique destiny, the politicians' cynical, duplicitous speeches, the spiteful faces of their supporters, the religious obscurantism, the jingoistic hysteria and the rest of this North Korea-style lunacy; but all that sits alongside a life that is otherwise quite normal – harmless, peaceful, fashionable, even cosmopolitan. A girl in big yellow headphones listening to the Arctic Monkeys skateboards past a billboard with pictures of ballistic missiles on it. It's called 'cognitive dissonance' and thank God it exists – that the counterculture still offers something, that it isn't all lost without a trace in a morass of TV propaganda. With that in mind, I asked my eldest daughter Sonia, who is 17, to provide a brief introduction to the subcultures of todays' Russia – the ones that she knows far better than I do. There are words in her report that I won't pretend to understand.

Young people nowadays want to stand out. If someone is absolutely ordinary they are seen as a complete failure: do you really not have the imagination to be a bit different? The more a young person is a mysterious non-conformist – a thinker, a cynic or a wannabe lad (not a good look) – the more 'karma points' they have and the more followers on social media, which is where people like them spend most of their time.

But as that modern-day philosopher Sergei Shnurov (the lead singer of the band Leningrad) rightly says, the ways of standing out are all clichés: tattoos, Converse sneakers, indie music, longboards, coffee from some secret new place – the same, obvious, superficial ideas that millions of people have. As they said in The Incredibles*: if everyone's unique, then no one's unique.*

Still, some young guys and girls manage somehow to seem relatively unclichéd, although it's increasingly rare. I thought I'd take it upon myself to list some of the contemporary subcultures that I come across (less in real life and more online) and describe them a bit. It's pretty subjective, admittedly, but this is how I see it as someone of the same age as these people, but looking in from the outside.

- Hipsters: skinny guys with beards and glasses who love coffee and pretentious, but superficial, conversations about anything and everything that's a bit 'different'. The more like tramps they look, the more different they think they are.
- Tumblr girls (and, more rarely, Tumblr boys): mummy's little nightmares, covered in stickers and glitter, rolling their eyes seductively and licking something long and spiky (calling Dr Freud!). On camera, of course.
- Football hooligans: a subtype of gopnik that lives and dies for Stone Island clothes and his crew, and generally sucks at school. They have a lot in common with skinheads and are mostly right-wing, pro-Putin patriots. But they don't talk about politics the whole time. They mostly hang out in playgrounds or at stadiums and drink beer and cheap energy drinks.
- Feminists: not all that different from Tumblr girls, but foaming at the mouth to prove that men are rapists, freaks, sexists and generally unnecessary – but also wanting people to treat them as they do men. Found pretty much exclusively online. It's better not to talk to them in case they suddenly get 'triggered'!

- *Ponyfuckers (aka Bronies): sensitive young guys with pink spots (just like Pinkie Pie) who watch* My Little Pony *with almost sexual fascination, quietly fantasising about Fluttershy.*
- *Weeaboos: anime fans who go around plastered in badges and wearing beaten-up cat's ears. They only interrupt their constant meowing to yell out whatever random Japanese words they know.*
- *Binge-watchers: people who obsess over foreign TV shows like Sherlock, Mr Robot and Shameless, and then inundate everyone with stupid tweets about the latest death / wedding / gay love interest. The real hardcore of this group now watch Ukrainian TV series.*
- *Hikkies or /b/tards: amoral, misanthropic online cynics, typically under 15 years old. For some reason they're all really into atheism and black humour. Most hikkies (the word comes from the Japanese hikikomori, meaning social recluse) are just wannabes hanging around image boards like 4chan and its Russian spinoff 2ch. Completely crazy and not put off by anything, not even sadism or child porn. Some of them are pretty handy hackers.*
- *Geeks: they hang out at so-called 'anti-cafes' (where you pay for your time, not your coffee) using free consoles and board games. You can also find them at comic book shops and Comic-Con Russia. Pretty similar to ponyfuckers, except they fantasise about Ahsoka Tano from* Star Wars *or Wendy Corduroy from* Gravity Falls. *A lot of the subtypes listed above – binge-watchers, weeaboos, ponyfuckers and, to an extent, Tumblr girls – started as geeks.*
- *Ravers: unhinged, hardcore pissheads who move between strangers' flats using their mum's metro card. They get wasted and then sleep until three in the afternoon.*

That's just a short list of the groups I have come across. I did see an emo on the metro the other day, but he disappeared pretty quickly. He must have realised that it wasn't 2007 anymore.

Unfortunately, all these subcultures have been borrowed from the West; but in the way the members of all these subcultures look and behave, there's still always an element of what Pelevin called "pure old-fashioned Russian fucked-up-ness". As far as entirely Russian subcultures go, there's really only the Putinists, which is more of a political organisation. Many subcultures are partly politicised. Lots of hikkies are armchair generals who lord it up discussing global geopolitics before their mums tell them to get off the computer. The feminists slag off any patriarchal country where women aren't respected enough, and they crush on female politicians. The binge-watchers whine about how great the West is with its amazing TV shows whereas everything in Russia is shit. But by and large the rest couldn't care less about politics.

It's very interesting to observe their behaviour from afar when these different groups come into contact with each other. Hooligans, for instance, can't stand geeks – and the feeling is mutual.

In conclusion, I should say that I myself have been a member of lots of different tribes: I've been a hippie and an emo and a goth and a weeaboo. Only now, though, have I realised: it doesn't matter what subculture you belong to (if you even belong to one), the most important thing is that you think and act as a free, intelligent individual guided by your own moral principles. But that's another story.

While I value Sonia's irony and her critical eye, I'd like to point out that "free, intelligent, moral individuals" feel better and stronger in groups of likeminded people – that is, subcultures – however comical they may appear from the outside. It's these groups who, in different countries and in different eras, have always been the agents of change. But the challenges facing these agents have been different – in Russia more than almost anywhere. In this country, before we can gather together the materials necessary to build the bright, shiny home of the future, we first of all need to break free, to emancipate ourselves, to smash the ice that entombs us – that is the heroic task that generations of Russians have been tackling for centuries.

With sadness I survey our present generation!
Their future seems so empty, dark, and cold,
Weighed down beneath a load of knowing hesitation,
In idleness stagnating, growing old.
We have received, when barely finished weaning,
The errors of our sires, their tardiness of mind,
And life oppresses us, a flat road without meaning,
An alien feast where we have dined.
T'ward good and evil shamefully uncaring
We wilt without a fight when starting on life's race;
When danger threatens us – ignoble want of daring,
Before those set on high – despicable and base.

(*Meditation*. Poem by Mikhail Lermontov.
Translation by Alan Meyers in *An Age Ago: A Selection of Nineteenth Century Russian Poetry*)

So begins a poem written by Mikhail Lermontov in 1838. In school they taught us that this great work, composed when Lermontov was only 24, was about the superfluous men. It's not hard to see that it works just as well for the youth of Russia today – the superficial *popsa* kids distressed at the economic downturn, the thuggish *gopniks* dying their ignominious early deaths from drugs and alcohol, the drilled ranks of pro-Putin conformists, and even the praiseworthy volunteers, the helpers who are helpless in the face of the repressive bureaucratic machinery of the state.

Yes, you get the feeling that we have been thrown back in time to the century before last – hence the mentions in the last chapter of the Decembrists, the People's Will and the superfluous men. It's a cycle, a spiral even. People say that democracy has never worked in Russia, and they're right. That's because democracy has never been tried in Russia. Even in the infamous Nineties, all we had was democratic window dressing for a system dominated by bureaucrats and gangsters. In Russia, history has always been made by a particular minority, while the majority of the population looked on and said nothing. Most often this minority has been stupid and malevolent; much more rarely, it has included wonderful people. Wonderful young people. That was what the Populist Nikolai Mikhailovsky was writing about in his 1882 article "Heroes and the Crowd": "A hero is not someone who performs some great feat. A hero is simply the first person to 'break through the ice', to make the decisive step that the crowd has been waiting for nervously, which will make them charge in one direction or another with rapid force. The hero is not important in himself, but only as a product of the mass movement that he calls forth." And so, right now, when it comes to changing Russia, all my faith lies with a dynamic, radical minority. With the young and the prepared. That's why I've paid so much attention in the past year to the artist Pyotr Pavlensky – a hero right out of *What is to be Done*, a 'new man' for our era.

But even a man as brave as Pavlensky has grown scared – above all for his two small children, who would be taken to a home if he were arrested – and in late 2016 he and his family emigrated to France. No country for young men? No more heroes? No future? Russia is indeed going through a dark period, but no government is capable of extinguishing hope entirely.

I see hope in the young activist Ildar Dadin, who stands alone in Putin's gulag raging against a repressive system. I see it in the guys from the Anti-Corruption Foundation, hackers and lawyers constantly risking not just their careers but also their freedom as they investigate the illegal enrichment schemes of the Kremlin elite. I see hope in the work of Mikhail Khodorkovsky's Open Russia project, a social education endeavour backing young politicians and professionals. I see hope in the schoolchildren who came out in their thousands in 2017 to protest against corruption.

I remember the early 1980s: then, too, everything seemed bleak and hopeless. In some ways it's better now: there are more options, and there is more information and more room for manoeuvre than there was in the totalitarian USSR. In other ways it's worse: nowadays, people lack the motivation we had, having experienced the bitter and disheartening experience of the defeat of freedom. But there's one thing I know for sure: if you look for it, you can find a way out of any dead end – and there are people who right now are searching for that way out. Russia rarely makes you happy, but it can always surprise you.

And surprise us it did on 26 March 2017. On that day a protest against corruption was called by the opposition leader Alexei Navalny. And young people turned up. In droves. Tens of thousands of very young people – schoolchildren and students – took to the streets. They made up the majority of the protests, which was more than a surprise, it was a real shock to everyone – to both the authorities and to representatives of the traditionally disgruntled dissidents of the intelligentsia and middle class. Loud and carefree, they chanted slogans against officials, climbed onto streetlights and brandished the symbols of anti-corruption memes. Protesters held aloft trainers and toy ducks, jibes aimed at former president, sneaker-fan and duckhouse-enthusiast Dmitry Medvedev, whose expensive tastes had been revealed in an exposé by Navalny. The atmosphere at these protests was utterly different to what came before: instead of the gloomy stoicism of recent efforts, there was a joyous, feisty celebration of disobedience. Of course, social media played a key role in coordinating this. What's more, in some cities around Russia – there were protests in more than 80 Russian cities on 26 March – the protests were initiated by young people, with no involvement from adults. One such organiser, from the tiny town of Pogar a few hours south of Moscow, was 16-year-old schoolboy Maxim Losev, who ended up being arrested at his school, right in the middle of a lesson.

I asked a famous Russian sociologist, Professor Alexei Levinson, whether the polls had predicted the sensational events of 26 March. They hadn't, he replied honestly. In fact he said that the results of sociological surveys showed young people to be the most conformist section of Russian society – apathetic and willing to support whoever was in power. On 12 June it was the same story. This time 150 cities had protests, in all of which teenagers predominated. In Moscow and St Petersburg the police reacted viciously, detaining 1,750 people. As one of the arrested teenagers said, "It's better to do 15 days in prison than live on many more years in this poverty."

The main slogan of these protests has been "Russia Without Putin". It's amazing how the 'first free generation', the children of the Nineties and Noughties on whom so many hopes were laid, turned out to be so unsuited to opposition, readily exchanging freedom and dignity for money and fun. A real generation of fighters was born in the teens of this century, during the years of reactionary Putinism, of Orthodoxy, patriotism and militarism. In Russia, it seems, everything happens not because of, but in spite of something; the spirit of freedom is fostered not in the nurseries of liberalism, but in the deserts of hopelessness. It's not for nothing that years ending in 17 have a special significance for Russians. Somehow or other, intangible hope has taken on real flesh, a movement has begun, the page has been turned and, perhaps, youth protest is again about to write another chapter in the history of Russia.

I'd like to close this book with a famous bit of dialogue from Bertholt Brecht's *Life of Galileo* (a great favourite back in the Soviet Sixties).

Andrea: Unhappy the land that has no heroes!

Galileo: No. Unhappy the land that needs heroes.

If you ask me, they're both right. Whichever way you look at it, Russia is not a happy country, and rarely has been. I don't know what's to blame — some inherited defect, bad karma or an unhappy accident, perhaps. Of course Russia needs heroes. Without them, there would be no flashes of light in the darkness. Fortunately, they do come: one by one, in passionate groups of conspirators or in happy bands. And while they are young, they feel no fear. So, when our corner of the globe at last gets its share of peace and harmony (here's hoping), our happy descendants will raise a glass to them — to the passionate and the peculiar.

'Russia will be free!'
Protests in St Petersburg.
Timur Khadzhibekov (Georgiy Markov), June 12, 2017.
Courtesy of the photographer

SUBKULTURA:
stories of youth and resistance in Russia 1815–2017
by Artemy Troitsky

First co-published in the United Kingdom in 2017:
The New Social, London and HOME Publishing, Manchester

On the occasion of the exhibition:
The Return of Memory
Friday 20th October 2017 – Sunday 7th January 2018

HOME
2 Tony Wilson Place
First Street, Manchester
M15 4FN, United Kingdom
www.homemcr.org

The exhibition: The Return of Memory
Curated by Olya Sova, Anya Harrison and Sarah Perks

Artists: AZA Shadenova, The Bureau of Melodramatic Research,
Declan Clarke & Sarah Perks, X-Ray Audio, Phil Collins, Callum Cooper,
Gluklya, Moon Kyungwon & Jeon Joonho, Victoria Lomasko,
Vladislav Mamyshev-Monroe, Evgeny Nikiforov, Marta Popivoda,
Ruslan Vashkevich and Irina Korina